The Success Manual For Adult College Students

How to go to college (almost)
full time in your spare time....
and still have time to hold down a job,
raise a family, pay the bills,
and have some fun!

Third Edition

**Visit our website at
http://www.adultstudents.com**

The Success Manual For Adult College Students

Copyright ©2006 Mike Doolin

10-Digit ISBN 1-59113-898-1
13-Digit ISBN 978-1-59113-898-3

Published by Michael J. Doolin, Rochester, NY, USA

Cover Design: Julie Sartain

All rights reserved. No part of this publication may be reproduced, stored in a retrieval system, or transmitted in any form or by any means, electronic, mechanical, photocopying, recording or otherwise, without the written permission of the author.

Any trademarks or logos used herein are the property of their respective owners.

Printed in the United States of America.

Booklocker.com, Inc.
2006

The Success Manual For Adult College Students

How to go to college (almost)
full time in your spare time....
and still have time to hold down a job,
raise a family, pay the bills,
and have some fun!

by Mike Doolin

Third Edition

Contents

Dedication vii
Acknowledgements ix
Foreword xi
Notes on the Second Edition xiii
Notes on the Third Edition xv
Introduction xvii
CHAPTER 1 Should You Even Go To College? 1
CHAPTER 2 Some Good Reasons To Go To College 6
CHAPTER 3 Conquering Your Fears 18
CHAPTER 4 Getting Yourself Organized and Finding The Support You Need 33
CHAPTER 5 How Fast Can You Actually Get A Degree? 50
CHAPTER 6 What Kind Of A Degree Do You Really Need? ... 57
CHAPTER 7 Who's Paying For All This? How To Find The $$$! 63
CHAPTER 8 Save A Ton of Money - Start At Your Local Community College 81
CHAPTER 9 How To Save Even More Money 89
CHAPTER 10 Budgeting 103
CHAPTER 11 Time Management 111
CHAPTER 12 Make Sure You Know What You Have To Take Before You Actually Take It 128
CHAPTER 13 How Adults Learn 143
CHAPTER 14 Take This Learning Style Inventory and Get To Know How You Learn 153
CHAPTER 15 Start Slow, Start Smart 173
CHAPTER 16 Chopping That 120 Credit Hour Goal Down To Manageable Size: Not All Of Your Credits Have To Come From The Classroom 179

CHAPTER 17 Online Learning	193
CHAPTER 18 What About Those Classes That I Absolutely Have To Take But Aren't Offered When And How I Need Them?	204
CHAPTER 19 Work Ahead	210
CHAPTER 20 Get To Know Your Teachers	214
CHAPTER 21 Dealing With The Bureaucracy	222
CHAPTER 22 Campus Resources	233
CHAPTER 23 Grades, Grading And Grade Point Averages	245
CHAPTER 24 Recheck Your Records Every Semester	258
CHAPTER 25 The Importance Of Having A Private Place To Study	263
CHAPTER 26 Studying And Note-Taking	271
CHAPTER 27 Writing	282
CHAPTER 28 Taking And Passing Tests	289
CHAPTER 29 Personal Computer, Yes Or No?	302
CHAPTER 30 Day Care	306
CHAPTER 31 Do You Have Time For A Social Life?	318
CHAPTER 32 What Are You Waiting For?	324
Reference	326
On-Line Resources	331
Organizations	333
Other ways to get credit	334
Veteran's Information	336

Dedication

This book is dedicated to all the adult students who are busting their butts trying to finish college, help take care of a family, hold down a job and still stay sane. Hang in there: you can do it. And it's worth it.

And to those adults who are just thinking about going to college: do it! It'll be the best thing you've ever done, for your family, for your career....but mostly for yourself.

To Ann, who makes all things possible.

To my daughters, Maura, Kelly, Shannon and Erin, for growing up cool.

To my granddaughters Alex, Stephie and Ally, my grandsons AJ and Nate, and my unknown gender grandchild due in April 2006: try to grow up as cool as your moms.

Acknowledgements

A book this comprehensive is not a one-person job. I couldn't have completed this project without a lot of help. Specific thanks to....

The adult students at Monroe Community College in Rochester, NY, Nazareth College in Pittsford, NY, the State University of New York in Brockport, NY and State University of New York Empire State College who were kind enough to take time out of their very busy schedules to be interviewed and talk at length about how they were completing college.

Ann Tippett, Betty Smith, Patty Ornt and Bill Sigismond at Monroe Community College.

The faculty and staff at Monroe Community College, and specifically everyone in Advising and Counseling, Transfer and Placement and Admissions. And big thanks to all my friends in the Advisement Center.

The thousands of adult students that I have talked with and advised at Monroe Community College and other schools around the country who made suggestions about what this book should contain.

Sister Monica Weis at Nazareth College.

Karla Merrifield and Roger Weir at the State University of New York at Brockport.

Dave DuBois, Nancy Gadbow, Sharon Grigsby, Herb Shapiro and Wayne Willis at the State University of New York Empire State College.

Foreword

April, a long time ago: I'm sitting in the principal's office with my parents, unceremoniously being tossed out of high school one day after my 17th birthday. Happy birthday, jerk! It's near the end of my Junior year. But it feels more like the end of my life. I've just joined the world's largest fraternity of losers: the high school drop-outs. The world is not a very nice place.

April, many years later: Another school, another place. My parents are here too...along with my wife and four daughters. The graduating class of a medium-sized midwestern university is filing across the stage in the field house to pick up their diplomas. And I'm right there in line with all the 21-year-old kids to get mine. I'm obviously very late getting it. But that piece of paper is in my hand, and that's all that matters to me. The world is a much nicer place.

In the very many years it took me to go from high school dropout to college graduate, I've memorized the physical layouts of nearly a dozen campuses in seven states, from Hawaii to New York. I've been a Psych major, an English major, a Sociology major, a General Business major, a Marketing major, and, finally, an Advertising major. I've dropped nearly as many classes as I ultimately finished and received credit for. I've taken a number of classes again, and again, and again, and yet again, because I kept changing colleges (and states and accreditation organizations) and the credits never transferred. And I've quite literally spent more time in classrooms than most people with PhDs.

By anyone's standards that's a lot of mistakes, a lot of backtracking. But in that very long trip through a college education I've learned more <u>about</u> the college system than in it. You <u>can</u> get a degree when you're over 30 or 40 (or even 50, 60 or 70!), married or in a relationship, working full-time, raising kids, paying mortgages, etc. etc.

Now, many years later and with a graduate degree, I find myself in the ironic position of *teaching* adult students in my local community college. And I do a lot of advising in this school, concentrating mainly on returning adult students. Every year I help hundreds of adult students return to college or continue in it, and their experiences and concerns have been incorporated into this third edition.

And as a result of this book and my website (http://www.adultstudents.com), I have launched a completely unexpected career as a public speaker and consultant! I have been invited to appear and speak at colleges and universities, and talk with adult student groups and college administrators about my favorite topic, which is, of course, adult students.

This is a "how to" book. It's intentionally short on theory, long on practice. It's full of the mistakes I made and some advice on how to avoid making them yourself. And it includes the experiences, advice and mistakes of a number of other adult college students too. It'll show you the strategies that work...and the ones that don't. It tells you the things you need to do and say, and the people to say and do them to. It shows you the pitfalls and traps to watch out for and how to avoid the most common problems. And it'll help make your trip to that degree faster and less painful than it might be.

And, perhaps most important of all, it'll help you develop the personal organization you absolutely must have to get a college education while your life is full of a lot of other responsibilities.

Right this minute, more than *7.5 million people* over the age of 25 are working on a college degree. This is about *half* of all college students in the country. And every year, tens of thousands of these adults - who are raising kids and working and trying to maintain a relationship and busy with hundreds of other details of life - manage to get a college degree. You can too. It certainly won't be as much fun as having mom and dad pay the freight when you were 18. And you probably won't be able to hang around dorms, drink a lot and party more.

But it can be done. And you're one of the ones who can do it.

Notes on the Second Edition

I originally wrote this book in a slightly different form as my Master's thesis in 1998, and it was published something over a year later. At the time I wrote it, it was pretty complete, and I was happy with its content.

I have earned a living writing since the mid-60s, mostly business materials like advertising, PR, magazine articles, web sites, brochures, manuals, etc. I started teaching business communications and technical writing courses part-time at Monroe Community College (MCC) in Rochester, NY in 1998 – mostly night school classes populated largely by returning adult students – and started making notes about changes and additions that I wanted to make to the book. College bookstores, including MCC, started selling the book, and many of the students who turned up in my night school classes bought it and had comments and suggestions, and I noted those as well. More than a few tracked me down and called or wrote or left emails on my website, www.adultstudents.com.

Shortly after I started teaching at MCC I started taking classes and seminars at the school designed to train me to become an adviser to adult students, and by the following year I started doing that part-time, in addition to teaching. My involvement in advising grew stronger every year, and by the year 2000 I was spending many hundreds of hours a year in the school's Advisement Center and advising hundreds of students every year, many of them returning adults.

Advising was a great opportunity to do more research on returning adults and get more ideas for the book, and I continued to make notes on ways to improve it. By the spring of 2003 I had lots of new material that I wanted to add and areas that I wanted to improve and I went to work.

The book you have in your hands – the Second Edition – has been considerably updated from the first in many ways, the most notable in the area of web sites. I have added dozens of sites to the text, and if you bought this book in its electronic form you should be able to just click through to those sites and access their information directly. The fact that this book is available in electronic form is also new: the First Edition was only available in a printed format.

I have also added more information about the advising process, its importance, and its place in your planning. As I teach more and advise more, I become more and more convinced that an hour or two with an experienced adult student adviser in your school can save you huge amounts of time, money and aggravation, by guiding you to the right classes and perhaps helping you find ways to earn credit outside of a classroom.

In the five years since I wrote the First Edition, I have personally known dozens more adult students who took that first step, contacted their local college, and started working toward that degree. I have had the pleasure of watching a number of them cross that stage with that coveted piece of paper in their hand, and I am delighted to be able to tell you that I helped them do that in some small way, by encouraging them to start, helping them choose appropriate majors and classes, and – in a number of instances – helping them become better writers in my writing classes.

The number of adult students continues to rise every year. With the huge expansion of on-line learning and more and more colleges catering to the adult student, there is more opportunity than ever to earn that degree when you're on the sunny side of 30, 40, 50 or older. (Just the other day I advised a woman who was just starting college at age 69!) If you've always had the dream of a college education,
you've made a good start by buying this book. Read it, then buy some of the others noted in the Reference section. Call your local college and make an appointment with an adult student adviser. Attend one of their orientation sessions

Then register for a class. Millions of adult students have gone back to school and gotten their Associate's, Bachelor's, Master's, even Doctorates.

You can too.

Mike Doolin
September 2003

Notes on the Third Edition

The revision on this edition began almost as soon as the Second Edition was published. Adult education is a hot topic, and it seems as if more and more people are paying attention to it, publishing more information about it, and, of course, actually doing it.

This edition reflects more of the changes going on in this field. Notable is the new chapter dealing with online learning. The growth in this area has been explosive in the last couple of years, and I have talked with literally hundreds of students, advisers and administrators about this topic.

Although that is the major change in this 3rd edition, dozens of smaller changes have been inserted here and there. All of the web site links have been checked and, where necessary, updated. Those few errors that somehow managed to creep into the last version have been corrected. And here and there I have added references to my web site (www.adultstudents.com), mostly in response to some readers of previous editions who happened on it accidentally and wondered why I never mentioned it in the book.

If you are in school right now, congratulations. Keep going. It'll be worth it. If you are just thinking about it, find a way to do it. It will be the most constructive, most marvelous thing you ever do.

And if you are an adult who has recently finished college, find someone who is still just thinking about it and buy them a copy of this book. Or give them your old copy. But help them make the decision. You already know it can change their life, just as it has changed yours. And mine.

Mike Doolin
March 2006

Introduction

> "I'm finally fulfilling my dream. I always wanted to go back to school."
> *Bette B., 40, married with two children, earned her Associate's degree and went on for her Bachelor's.*

So, here you are: somewhere between 25 and 125

Perhaps you're married or in some other type of relationship, and maybe there's one or more children around. Along with a mortgage payment or rent, car payment, credit card payment, a full or part-time job, some friends you'd like to see once in awhile and a bunch of other responsibilities.

Welcome to adulthood and the middle class.

You'd like to finish (or even start) college. But you know it would be tough to just quit working for four or more years and go to college with the 18-year-old kids. Somehow you missed your chance at a college education years ago, and the best you can hope for now is that somehow you'll be able to help your kids get their college education.

But it's too late for you, right?

Wrong!

According to U.S. Census data (The Big Payoff: Educational Attainment and Synthetic Estimates of Work-Life Earnings, July 2002: http://www.census.gov/prod/2002pubs/p23-210.pdf, only about 26% of the U.S. population over 25 years old currently has a Bachelor's Degree.

But common sense tells you that there are lots of people - millions of people - who are fully capable of handling college-level work. For one reason or another a lot of very bright individuals never got a chance to go to college when they were younger and less encumbered with responsibilities. Maybe you were one of them.

Perhaps your family couldn't afford to send you. Maybe you did badly in high school and would have never been accepted to a college. Maybe, like me, you didn't even finish high school. Or maybe you actually did start college, but dropped out for some reason, with the intention of returning later.

There was a time - not that long ago - when you would have been permanently consigned to the uneducated if you didn't go into college right out of high school. Colleges were specifically designed and run to cater to the 18 - 21-year-old day-school-student crowd. Anyone who happened to be much older than that, say 30 or, God forbid, 40, 50 or 60, or who happened to be occupied during the day with an insignificant little activity like earning a living to support his or her family, was out of luck. Night school and weekend courses were almost non-existent, and most other ways to get college credit – like online classes - hadn't even been invented. Community colleges were equally rare. And college personnel in general were almost unable to conceive of an undergraduate student old enough to legally drink.

> **"Going back to school has really helped. I know I can do it now. I've done so well here at school."**
> *Deanne L., 39, married with two kids, started school when she was 19. She was 40 when she earned her Bachelor's degree.*

College isn't just for the kids anymore
Fortunately for all of us in the almost-over-the-hill crowd, a lot has changed. Colleges have discovered that there are millions of people who would take classes if those courses were offered at times, in places and in ways that were convenient to us older, working, married, parenting, mortgage-paying folks. And in addition to those more convenient classes, they've created ways to get college credit that don't even require you to sit in a classroom. (It's kind of ironic that if the college administrators had ever taken any of the Marketing classes their Business Departments were offering, they would have spotted this huge potential market decades before they actually did.)

Unfortunately for the older student, this shift in thinking is still not complete. It is still not easy for the so-called "non-traditional" student (that's us working, over-25 folks) to get a degree. Many colleges continue to focus on the day school student. And while many schools do offer a large selection of night school, weekend and distance-learning classes, a lot of these classes are not systematically integrated into a coherent, comprehensive adult student program. And even in schools which do have a good selection of courses for us non-traditional students, there is seldom a separate, fully-staffed department specifically designed to help the older, part-time, working student handle all of his or her problems in getting a degree.

And there is still a large adjustment to be made in the attitudes of faculty and administration alike toward the older student. We are just not like those young kids they see in classes every day, and the people who run the schools and teach the classes sometimes don't quite know what to make of us older students. We act differently, we study differently, we work differently. And we learn differently. And we tend to place different demands on the educational system and have much different expectations of it.

And in many cases the system fails us completely.

Mike Doolin

Bookstores that close at 4 PM are fine for the kids in the dorms. But they don't do you much good if you don't get out of work til 5 PM. Ditto for admissions, advising and counseling offices with office hours only during the day, and libraries, labs and computer facilities that get locked at 6 PM. Parking lots that are vacant at night but can't be used by part-time students. Courses which are scheduled and then cancelled without so much as a phone call. Book requirements that get changed at the last minute. These are the types of things that drive night school and other non-traditional students up the wall.

Now add in professors who have never held down a real job in a factory or office and just don't understand why the demands of earning a living or paying attention to a family sometime take precedence over schoolwork. Reading, homework and term paper assignments that are designed more to keep the day school kids off the streets and out of the bars than to contribute any real knowledge to you. Textbooks and courses that have little real practical value. Courses you are probably qualified to teach but can't test out of. Graduation requirements which include courses that are only offered during times when most adult students can't take them.

And so forth.

No matter where you go to college, if you're an older, working, non-traditional student type, you can count on running into problems like these with regularity. For the most part, the educational system has not yet completely assimilated the non-traditional student, and it hasn't been completely redesigned to account for your peculiar situation.

The educational system *is* working on it. But it's not there yet.

A good share of this book will flag you to those areas you should pay careful attention to, and the problems you might have just because you are an older, part-time student. There are a lot of techniques and ploys in here to help you circumvent or at least deal with the minor and major irritations of trying to get through school, along with a lot of suggestions on how to get college credit without ever going near a college. And there's information about how to get - and stay - organized for the college experience, without going broke, crazy, or through a divorce.

All of the strategies and tactics outlined here have worked for me, the many students I interviewed for this book, and the hundreds of adult students I've seen over the years in my role as an adviser at my local community college and the many others I have had the pleasure of talking with at the colleges and universities I've visited as a guest speaker and consultant.

I can't claim personal credit for inventing much of what's here. These ideas and concepts have been conceived by people just like you and me, people who simply wanted to get a college education but kept running into problems that they had to solve - personal problems, problems with the college system and the ways it allowed them to earn credit, problems with their social and family lives, problems with their work environments, problems with paying for school, problems in managing their limited time. What you read here is what those people did to solve those problems and get that college credit.

But if the ideas were often conceived in frustration, they were executed out of necessity, always in desperation, and many times in sheer panic. Panic is defined - as one example - as that feeling you get when a college administrator tells you, a week before graduation, that you are not going to graduate because you didn't take a phys ed course several years earlier that some other administrator told you you didn't have to take because your military service could substitute for it.

That actually happened to me.

> "I didn't have a lot of self-confidence for a lot of years, and the successes that I've had in school have made me think a lot better of myself."
>
> *Karen D., a 46 year old single mother of 4, started college in the 1970s. It took her nearly 25 years to earn her Bachelor's Degree.*

College is a different world for adults

Make no mistake. From the moment you decide to get a college education on a part-time basis and still hold down a job, stay in a relationship, help raise children and try to enjoy a reasonably normal life, you enter a totally alien world. Like the surface of the moon, much of the college system was never designed to be inhabited by people like you. To survive your experience in the hallowed halls of learning, you had better be prepared.

You will be unknown, unloved, unrecognized, and - when the computer screws up, as it surely will - unaccounted for. Your emotional stability will be constantly tested, your ego punched, pushed, pummeled and preyed-upon. Your social life will disintegrate, your love life will become erratic, and you will become a stranger to your mate and children. You will probably spend much more money on the pursuit of the degree than you ever estimated. And it may take you much longer to finish it than you ever thought possible.

Your physical appearance will become that of a person who sleeps too little and has suspect nutritional habits. You will become a source of concern to those you love you. Your personal habits will become unpredictable.

And the use of your precious time will be almost completely dictated by faceless educational barbarians in the halls of learning who neither know nor care what they are doing to you.

(Is this beginning to sound like a lot of fun?)

You will be faced with impossible decisions nearly every day, confronted with situations that would test the patience of an angel, and barraged by advice from well-meaning but completely clueless people who haven't the vaguest idea of what you are going through.

You will spend years camped on the enemy's doorstep, and you will be required to make regular sorties into his territory to attend classes, do research, use facilities or unsnarl red tape. He will know you are there, and he will tolerate your presence only when it suits him. He will fire on you at random intervals from totally unexpected directions. You must be ready to react instantly and appropriately, for he is better trained, better armed.

He will cheerfully cancel classes, change requirements, lock facilities, issue parking tickets, provide fraudulent advice, publish incorrect information, lose records and provide you with countless other ways to become confused and discouraged. And he'll do it all with a smile on his face and a song in his heart, while he tap-dances, Fred Astaire-style, across every one of your carefully planned maneuvers to get to that degree.

He doesn't think of himself as your enemy, but as your friend. And that makes him even more dangerous. View him and his campus with a healthy dose of suspicion. Question his motives. Check and recheck his information. Never forget that you are in his land. He makes the rules.

You were armed for this war at birth with common sense. You've honed your survival skills over years of being a spouse or partner, a parent, an employee. You have fought and won countless battles that he - and his army of 18-year-old minions - have never experienced. You can be cunning, clever and creative in ways and at times that he can only dimly anticipate. And he will be totally powerless over some of your defenses.

And now you are almost ready to begin preparation for what will be a long series of small skirmishes and large battles. This book is Boot Camp, and you will soon become what you must be to get a college education when you're an adult, have a family and a job:

an adult college student success story!

> "I was starting out in community college with a lot of people who were 23, 24 years old. I felt that the system was designed for them. And of course I could do better. And I found that to be true."
>
> *Patrick A., 46 and the father of two small children, earned his Bachelor's degree in a little over five years, while still holding down a job.*

CHAPTER 1

Should You Even Go To College?

> "In the back of my mind was always that desire that someday I was going to get my college education because I deserved it."
> *Kathleen C., 56 and a grandmother, started college in the 1970s. It took her over 20 years to earn her Associate's Degree and six more to earn her Bachelor's Degree.*

Asking if you should even go to college may seem a strange way to begin this book

But it is a valid starting point. No matter how you do it - and there are any number of ways to earn college credit - getting a Bachelor's degree as an adult (and probably part time) is not an easy chore. It is going to cost you many thousands of dollars and years of your life. And although earning a degree has many positive benefits, going to college also has the potential to cause you a great deal of aggravation. View it as an investment: there is both risk and reward. Ask the same kind of questions you'd ask if you were going to buy a house.

Many people neither need nor want a house. Or, for that matter, a college education. They realize it, and decide to do something else with their time and money.

Many more <u>need</u> a house or a degree, but don't really <u>want</u> it. They understand that it is going to cost them a lot of time and money, but their situation is such that they really just can't do without it. So they go ahead with the project, bite the bullet, and just do it, sacrificing other things.

The third category is the people who <u>want</u> a degree (or a house), but don't really need it. It's more a matter of personal pride than anything else. Under this set of circumstances it becomes purely a private choice - there is no outside pressure from an employment or social standpoint that forces a person into college.

And finally, there are those who both <u>want and need</u> a degree.

Let's examine these categories. If you are reading this book you are in one of them. Determining which one you are in will help you answer the question that starts this chapter: Should you even go to college?

Some people need a degree but don't want it

A lot of people <u>need</u> a degree but don't really want it. More accurately, they don't really want to make the investment in time, money and energy required to get the degree. If degrees were free, these folks would probably take the diploma if it came in the mail. But if it didn't show up they wouldn't much care.

Most of the people in this category are working for some corporation that places a high value on a college degree and the formal, structured education that goes with it. If you don't have the piece of paper you aren't considered qualified to do certain jobs or fill certain positions...and earn the salaries that go with those jobs. End of discussion. Actual performance and innate talent don't have much to do with it.

I once worked with an electronics technician who had originally been trained in the military. He could only be described as brilliant. He had an obvious and awesome talent for electronic circuit design. And he was a much better circuit designer than almost all of the degreed electronics engineers in the department. Everybody knew it. But this guy had no chance of ever being promoted to (and being paid to be) an electronic design engineer, simply because he didn't meet the hiring criteria for that position: a BS degree in electronic engineering.

If this sounds like your situation, you have several choices. You can find another company to work for that places more emphasis on performance and less on pieces of paper, or you can prepare yourself to go nowhere in your career at your current company.

Or you can get your degree.

Those are your choices.

Some people want a degree but don't need one

There are also a lot of people who <u>want</u> a degree but don't really need it. Almost everyone who's self-employed or who runs his or her own business is in this category. Most skilled tradespeople fit here too. Ditto for the creative types who are already making a living as a writer, artist, musician, etc. While the information and learning that goes with earning a degree might be interesting to them, lack of a degree has no material effect on their ability to make a living, and no one is ever going to demand that they have one. So earning a Bachelor's degree is strictly a matter of personal choice. Many of these people actually do get degrees eventually. But they decide to go to college only as a matter of personal pride.

> **"I was divorced in the 90s and stayed home for a few years with the children. When my youngest was in kindergarten, I thought I would go back to the workforce and found out that the workforce was not ready for me. (So) I decided that I really needed to finish college so that I could support the children, regardless of child support."**
>
> *Karen D., 46 and the single mother of four, started school in the early 1970s. She earned a Bachelor's degree more than 25 years later and went on for her Master's.*

If you want and need a degree

And finally, there are those who both want and need a degree. These folks are probably working for the same companies as the people in the second category, except that they have decided that they are going to stay with that company and therefore have to have that piece of paper to move forward in their careers. Or, realizing that the days of lifetime employment with any employer are probably over, they decide to get a degree to enhance their employment and survival skills in the job market.

Should you get a degree?

Only you can answer that question. And it's a question that you need to truthfully answer to yourself before you decide to get that piece of paper.

But understand right up front that this college project is going to absorb staggering amounts of time, will disrupt your life as you currently know it, will probably take you years to complete, and may cost a ton of money.

Some of it - most of it, probably - will be great fun and very interesting. And the further you get into the process, the more you are likely to find it thoroughly rewarding. You'll meet a lot of very nice people and learn an enormous number of things....some of which you might even remember after the grade card comes in the mail. And your opinion of yourself will increase enormously.

But make no mistake:

- **It ain't gonna be easy**
- **It ain't gonna be quick, and**
- **It ain't gonna be cheap.**

This book will help you make it easier and quicker, and perhaps a bit less expensive. But even under ideal conditions you will wind up doing a lot of work.

It is a hell of a project.

But it can be done. And that is the main point of this entire book: it can be done. And it can be done by you.

> "I had wondered what it would be like to have a college degree but I hadn't really found a need for it. But the world has changed."
> *Patrick A., 46, married and the father of two small kids, finished his Bachelor's in five years while still working a part time job.*

CHAPTER 2

Some Good Reasons To Go To College

> "I knew that they were setting me up to lay me off so I decided that I would go. If they offered me that (severance) package then I would leave and go back to school full time."
>
> *Linda W., 41, started at a community college in the very late 70s, dropped out,, returned to that community college more than 15 years later, earned her Associate's Degree in four years and transferred to a private 4 year school. She earned her Bachelor's Degree a few years later.*

A changing workplace

It's no secret that the workplace in America is not the same as it used to be. In the 60s, 70s, even into the 80s, once you landed a job with a corporation - particularly a large, multinational blue chip company - you were pretty much assured of lifetime employment if you behaved yourself. And if you did your job reasonably well, you could generally count on periodic promotions and increases in pay.

At the end of maybe 30 or 40 years or so, they'd throw you a big party, give you a gold watch and send you a nice retirement check every month. And they would probably continue to pay for those expensive benefits like medical insurance, life insurance, etc. And you'd still be young enough (and hopefully healthy enough) to enjoy a number of years without the need to work every day.

Those days are gone.

Corporations these days seem to be much more interested in the bottom line and producing dividends for shareholders than they are in keeping employees, even the good, faithful employees who worked their butts off. No one's job seems safe. Many believe that this new era calls into question the entire concept of loyalty to a corporation. A lot of people have come to the conclusion that being devoted to a particular company is at least silly and probably even dangerous. It's every man and woman for themselves.

Whether that blanket indictment applies to you or not only you can decide. But just to be on the safe side you should probably be as well equipped as possible to make your own way in the employment market. These days you just don't know whether you're going to have a job tomorrow. You probably can't trust your employer, at least not many of them. Many employers large and small have shown a rather complete disregard for the welfare of their employees. Your company might be different. But the odds don't appear good.

What is a good bet is that sometime during your 40+ year working career you will be out of a job: the company changes direction and no longer needs your skills and fires you, it goes belly-up, is absorbed by another corporation that lets you go, working conditions become just intolerable and you quit.

It doesn't matter how it happens. One day you are employed, the next day you aren't. Where do you go from there?

> "I became disabled on my job working as a secretary in a law firm. ...My doctor told me to get into another line of work."
> *Evelyn S., 41, originally started college in 1975 and returned more than two decades later to work on her Bachelor's Degree. She eventually earned that and went on for her Master's.*

College graduates just have more options

If you have a college education you have a lot more employment possibilities than the person who does not have that education. Why? Because college graduates are in a minority - there just aren't that many of them. In general it's the college graduates who run this country (and the rest of the world) and the companies and organizations in it. If you are a college graduate you have a high probability of winding up as a manager, while those without a college education have a good chance of reporting to those of us who do. That's just the way the world is: education produces benefits.

On average, only about one person in four over the age of 25 graduates from college, as Table I shows. You are a relatively rare individual if you have a Bachelor's degree. And even rarer if you have a graduate degree. And that education makes you more valuable to a prospective employer.

TABLE I

EDUCATIONAL ATTAINMENT OF PEOPLE 25 YEARS OLD AND OLDER, BY SEX:

MARCH, 2000 (Numbers in thousands)*

Educational Attainment	Both Sexes Number	Both Sexes Percent	Male Number	Male Percent	Female Number	Female Percent
Total population 25+	175,230	100.0	83,611	100.0	91,620	100.00
None	851	0.48	396	0.47	455	0.51
Elementary: 1-4	1,891	1.08	945	1.13	945	1.03
Elementary: 5-6	3,542	2.02	1,738	2.08	1,804	1.97
Elementary: 7-8	5,896	3.36	2,839	3.40	3,057	3.34
High school: 1	3,680	2.10	1,761	2.11	1,919	2.09
High school: 2	4,975	2.84	2,276	2.72	2,700	2.95
High school: 3	7,019	4.00	3,261	3.90	3,759	4.10
High school grad	58,086	33.15	26,651	31.88	31,435	34.31
Some college, no degree	30,753	17.55	14,540	17.39	16,213	17.70
Associate degree: occupational program	7,221	4.12	3,224	3.86	3,998	4.36
Associate degree: academic program	6,471	3.69	2,729	3.26	3,742	4.08
Bachelor's degree	29,840	17.03	14,909	17.83	14,931	16.30
Master's degree	10,396	5.93	5,166	6.18	5,230	5.71
Professional degree	2,586	1.48	1,752	2.10	834	0.91
Doctorate degree	2,023	1.15	1,425	1.70	599	0.65

Source: U.S. Bureau of the Census, Current Population Reports, P20-536, *Educational Attainment of People 25 Years Old and Older*, March 2000 Current Population Survey.
http://www.census.gov/population/socdemo/education/p20-536/tab01.txt
* Note that this online link is updated periodically and the numbers you find there might differ a bit from those here. The ones on the internet are obviously more current.

If you are a professional - an engineer, a lawyer, a medical doctor, nurse, an accountant or some other licensed white collar worker - at least you have a good handle on what type of job you will be looking for. And you probably have an equally good idea of what type of organization hires your sort of person. You are pre-qualified for those new jobs by virtue of the fact that you have that particular degree.

Though probably not quite as well off as the professionals, those of us with a plain old Bachelor's degree are still pretty employable. We've learned how to do a lot of things in college, and potential employers know that.

The people who only got through high school have a much bigger problem in terms of their employment prospects. Not that it's ever easy for anyone, with any level of education, to get reestablished in the job market after being let go. It's not.

But people with college degrees - any kind of college degree - usually do better. They have already demonstrated to the world that they know how to set a goal and get to it. And that is particularly true for someone who can brag - yes, brag! - that they put themselves through college as an adult, one course at a time, often on their own nickel, and that they were willing and able to slog through that project, even though it took five, six, seven or more years.

What does that tell a prospective employer? For that matter, what does that positive, "I can do this" attitude tell your current employer?

> **"So I find that because I have more confidence, I've been able to put more of myself into all the work that I do - parenting work and my real job and all the other stuff that I do."**
> *Patrick A. finished his Bachelor's degree with a 3.6 GPA.*

Think about this. Being able to get through college at 30, 40, 50 or so, while raising a family and working, is a stunning personal accomplishment. It is one that no 22 year old recent graduate can brag about.

But you can.

And that makes you a better employee. Will that accomplishment keep you from getting fired? Maybe. If it comes down to choosing between you and someone who didn't do what you did, the odds probably favor you.

Will it automatically get you a new job if you are somehow turned loose from a company? There are no guarantees, of course. But being able to brag about how you went through school will definitely deliver some extra points in that job interview. It shows a level of perseverance and commitment to a goal that a lot of people just don't have.

Are job flexibility and future employability the only reasons to go to college? No. Although they are certainly important, the big reason for many people is money, pure and simple.

College graduates make a lot more money

The simple fact is that college graduates make more money than people with two-year degrees, who in turn make more money than people with high school educations. Some numbers are in order to support that.

TABLE II

Median Incomes of Various Educational Levels
Year-Round, Full-Time Workers
2001 Data (US Dollars)*

	Males	Difference from Previous Level		Females
		Male	Female	
Less than 9th grade	21,361			16,691
9th - 12th grade, no diploma	26,209	4,848	2,465	19,156
HS Grad (includes equivalency)	34,723	8,514	6,147	25,303
Some college, no degree	41,045	6,322	5,115	30,418
Associate degree	42,776	1,731	1,735	32,153
Bachelor's degree	55,929	13,153	8,841	40,994
Master's degree	70,899	14,970	9,675	50,669
Doctorate degree	86,965	16,066	11,454	62,123
Professional degree	100,000	13,035	-375	61,748

Source: U.S. Bureau of the Census, Current Population Reports, P60-series.
http://www.infoplease.com/ipa/A0883617.html
* Note that this online link is updated periodically and the numbers you find there might differ a bit from those here. The ones on the internet are obviously more current.

As of 2001 - the latest data available - a male who didn't get through high school had a median annual earning power of about $26,209, while a high school graduate could expect $34,723, about $8500 per year more. Someone with an Associate's degree could add about $8000 per year to that, bringing his median yearly income up to about $42,776. The figures for women, unfortunately, are lower, but the effect is the same: more education means more income.

> "When my husband's business started to fail I went out to work. My first job was working the B-shift in a factory. That was quite an eye-opener for me, to see women who had no choice. Working in a factory was all that they were equipped to do academically. And I thought, this isn't where I want to be."
>
> *Kathleen C. started college in 1971 and finally earned her Bachelor's degree nearly 30 years later.*

So far, so good. And that difference in earning power at the two-year college level is an excellent reason to officially get your two year, Associate's degree and go through the graduation line when you are halfway through school. It gives you something that proves you are halfway through. Being able to show that piece of paper is much stronger proof than merely saying "I have 60 credits."

Back to our example. If an Associate's degree is worth about $42,776 for a male and $32,153 for a female, then what is a Bachelor's degree worth?

Bachelor's degrees are worth more $$$$!
And the answer is, more...a <u>lot</u> more.

Males with Bachelor's degrees, on average, bring home $55,929, a huge $13,153 per year increase over the two year degree holders. For women the figures are $40,994 per year for a Bachelor's, a $8,841 per year advantage over Associate's degree holders. That puts a very high value on that extra two years of school. And for what it's worth, people with Master's degrees do significantly better, as you would expect: about $70,899 per year for males, $50,669 for females. And remember that these numbers are medians: half of the sample is above this level, half are below.

> **"When this fall comes and I get the job teaching, I'll have something that I've never had in my life, which is benefits. I'll have a steady acceptable paycheck. I've been waiting for 15 years for that."**
>
> *Patrick A., 46, worked as a waiter for many years before entering college. It took him a bit more than five years to earn his Bachelor's Degree – while working part time.*

If you'd rather work with ratios, here are some from the U.S. Census *Condition of Education, 2000 (see Section 2: Learner Outcomes: Economic Outcomes and Table 23-2. The entire report is at* http://nces.ed.gov/pubs2004/2004077.pdf*)*. The data is from 1998, the latest available.

Using a ratio of 1.00 as the standard for a high school graduate, a male who didn't finish high school could expect to earn just 0.75 of the pay of a high school graduate. If he had some college, his expected pay was 1.18 that of a high school graduate. And a Bachelor's degree gave him a 1.61 salary advantage over a high school graduate. The numbers for women are equally impressive: 0.76, 1.20 and 1.62. And a word of caution: these ratios are steadily getting wider. Since 1990, the earnings advantage of getting a Bachelor's degree has increased noticeably for both men and women. In that year, the ratios for men were 0.78, 1.19 and 1.48, and 0.79, 1.21 and 1.53 for women. The reverse of this is obviously just as true: people with less education are falling farther behind in the economic sweepstakes.

Looking at actual dollars (year 2001 figures, Census Bureau, Current Population Reports, Series P-60), if you are male you can expect a Bachelor's degree to add about $21,200 per year to your income if you graduated from high school and an additional $29,720 per year if you didn't finish high school. For females a Bachelor's will add $15,691 per year for high school grads and $21,838 per year for those who didn't finish high school.

Over an average working career of about 40 years, this will add up to an extra $848,000 to $1,188,800 in your pocket if you're a male, and $627,640 to $873,520 in your pocketbook if you're female. Pick up a Master's degree and you effectively double your earning power over a high school education over your working life.

Could you use an extra half a million to a million bucks....or maybe twice that with a Master's?

I thought so. If you're interested in the details, check Table II, compliments of the U.S. Bureau of the Census.

> **"I think it's more important that I'm headed toward a career instead of a job. I always saw my other jobs as just jobs, where the only thing I could really offer a company was that I could type really fast."**
>
> *Ann H., 33, spent more than ten years as a secretary before entering college. She eventually earned her Bachelor's degree.*

And it's not just money

Although most of us find the extra income from a college education pretty handy, there are a couple of other benefits from going to college. Learning new things, being exposed to new ideas, being able to put new concepts together - all can be pretty exciting once you start doing them. It's amazingly easy to get hooked on learning, and nearly every student I talked with for this book, and those hundreds I've talked with since were not going to stop with a Bachelor's degree. Most of them had plans for their Master's, and a number were shooting for a PhD. This attitude is pretty common. You'll find that once you start learning, you probably won't want to stop.

The final reason to finish that degree doesn't have anything to do with making more money or making you more employable or even the joy of continually learning new things. It has to do with how you feel about yourself.

When you finally stroll down that aisle and cross that stage and that college president hands you that piece of paper, you will feel very, very good about yourself. You will be absolutely, completely ecstatic. I guarantee it.

And something else: you'll be more self-assured, more confident than you've ever been. You'll know that you'll be able to learn and understand anything that you need to know. You'll be able to take on and complete big, complex projects that a lot of your friends would never tackle. You can sit in meetings with your head up and a smile on your face and no one - no one - will be able to successfully challenge your ability to get a big job done.

You already finished the biggest job of your life: you graduated from college as an adult. Everything else is small by comparison.

And PS: Spend the extra few hundred bucks and buy the biggest college ring you can afford and put that coveted sheepskin in the most expensive frame you can find and then hang it for all to see in your living room or right over your dining room table. You earned it.

> **"It will definitely improve my life, as well as my kids' too. Because of the simple fact that I'm in school now, and I'm also on public assistance."**
> *Joyce M., a 36 year old single mother of three, earned her Associate's and then her Bachelor's.*

CHAPTER 3

Conquering Your Fears

> **"Walking through those doors was the hardest thing I ever did."**
> *Evelyn S., married and the mother of two, originally started school in her late 20s. About 25 years later she earned her Bachelor's.*

The Fear Factor

This book is short on theory, long on practical advice. And, I hope, totally devoid of BS. So let's get the discussion of fear of college out of the way quickly.

Is there reason to be afraid of going to college as an adult? You bet there is.

And any book or person who tells you differently is full of it. You have a lot of very good reasons to be afraid of college. Nearly every adult student formally interviewed for this book mentioned that fear, and nearly every adult student I've ever known has been afraid. Every adviser and teacher I've talked with noted fear as a problem. I see it regularly in my school's Advisement Center when I work with adult students. I've seen it in the many students I've talked with in my travels to other campuses as a speaker and consultant. And I felt it myself, first when I did my Bachelor's work years ago, and much more recently when I started on my Master's degree. That fear is very real. And don't let anyone tell you that you don't feel it.

But just because it's real doesn't mean it can't be beaten. It can. Maybe not quickly. And maybe not every fear all at once. But like the rest of this huge project, beating back that fear is doable, one little piece at a time. Let's look at your fears, and try to put them into perspective.

> **"....a couple of days before the deadline to sign up I was in tears. I told my husband I couldn't do it and he kept on telling me, 'you have to have confidence in yourself. You can do it. You're bright, you can do it.' And I was just so afraid."**
> *Ann H., 33, married with one child, finally did do it: She graduated with a Bachelor's degree and a 3.75 GPA.*

Fear: My academic skills are shot.
I'll never be able to keep up with the requirements.

This is probably the most common fear: fear of failing, probably badly, probably in the public glare of a classroom, and definitely in front of your family and in a classroom full of people a lot younger. And while this fear sounds perfectly rational - you <u>have</u> been out of school a long time, you know! - it's nonsense. The evidence suggests just the reverse: that adult students are actually <u>better</u> students. And usually <u>much</u> better.

Ask virtually any college instructor who her best students are. The answer will almost invariably be: adult students. Ask any adult student you know how they're doing in school: most of them are doing just fine, thank you, and not a few of them are on the Dean's List, in the Honor Society or about to graduate with some special recognition. (This drives the younger students crazy, by the way! The presence of an adult student in a classroom full of younger students always sets the performance bar a lot higher than it would be if that adult student wasn't there.)

Don't believe it? Ask some typical, young college students who the best students in their classes are. The answer will probably be the same: adult students.

Need to see for yourself? Try these fear-conquering tactics:

Fighting the fear of failure

1. This entire book - and others like it - are dedicated to helping you succeed in college, by showing you (or reminding you) how to pick the right classes, take notes, study, pass tests, manage your time efficiently and so forth. Although going to college as an adult is a big project, it can be done. Many millions of adult students before you have done it. Seven or eight million more are in school right now. And most of them were just like you (and me): scared to death of failing.

Don't stop by reading this book - buy some of the others. Most of them are very good, and all of them have some positive advice to offer. There are several listed in the Reference section in the back of this book.

2. Go to your local college bookstore and browse through the textbooks being used in their courses. Most of them are very straightforward and easy to understand. And if you can comprehend the material while you're standing in a busy bookstore, imagine how much clearer and more interesting it will be when you have an expert at the front of the room helping you, and you have time to study and think about the material.

3. Find an adult student and take a look at the work they are doing. Look at their texts, their tests, their notes, the papers they write. This is not, as they say, brain surgery or rocket science. College courses are designed to accommodate average, ordinary people who work at an average rate with an average set of brains and skills. And college teachers are in the business of helping you acquire knowledge. They want you to learn. You can do this.

4. Find an interesting course and take it. Your local community college offers hundreds of courses on every conceivable topic, from English 101 to Tibetan Cooking. Pick a course that you think you'd find fun and interesting, and take it.

Or, if you think your local college might be too much of a challenge right now, find an Adult Ed course offered through your local public school system, or some other organization like a church or synagogue, a public service group or through a bookstore or library. Adult education is a huge business in this country. There are probably dozens, perhaps hundreds of courses available in your community. Find an interesting one and ace it. It'll do wonders for your confidence.

> **"I was afraid I wouldn't get the grades, I was afraid I wouldn't be accomplished. And I was afraid that I would be making a fool of myself."**
> *Evelyn S., 41, married with two kids, started college the first time in the mid-1970s. She dropped out. She returned more than two decades later and eventually graduated with a Bachelor's Degree and a GPA of 3.5.*

Fear: I know I can't read, write or do simple math well enough to do college level work.

Well, this might actually <u>be</u> true, but at this point you're really only guessing. Your skills might be just fine. And even if it is true, it's not a good reason to stop you. Skills can be improved, and sometimes it doesn't take very much to make a dramatic improvement in them.

Fighting the fear of inadequate skills

1. Your local college will be happy to give you a series of tests that can assess your skill levels in reading, writing and math. If your basic skills are a little weak - and don't be so quick to assume that - the college can recommend the sorts of courses you should take to get them back up to par. And there is an excellent chance that the college offers these courses.

2. Basic skills courses are widely available. Your local college, your city school district, your county, your state and private organizations like Literacy Volunteers all run them. And many of them are free or nearly free.

3. All bookstores and libraries have books on developing your skills. Check your librarian or an adviser at the organization where you took the skills tests for some recommendations.

> **"I never even got a high school diploma. All I have is a GED."**
> *Rich H., 44, finished his Bachelor's Degree in just 2-1/2 years. He worked full time, has six kids and a nearly perfect GPA.*

**Fear: I never graduated from high school.
How can I get into a college?**

Lots of people never successfully completed high school. The author of this book is one of them. And surprise! You don't need to graduate from high school to go to college if you're an adult. Virtually all community colleges will allow you to take classes without ever asking if you graduated from high school. They're not interested in what you did or didn't accomplish 10, 20 or 30 years ago - they want to know what you can do now. But if this still bothers you - even though it doesn't bother your college - here's some things you can do.

Fighting the fear of being a high school dropout
1. The GED (General Educational Development) Tests are widely available and regularly scheduled. A call to your city school district or college counseling office can get you the details. If you pass these tests - and there's no reason why you can't - you have a high school diploma that's recognized all over the country.
2. Many colleges have a program that automatically grants you a high school diploma if you successfully complete the first year of college work. Some require as little as 24 hours of successful credit.
3. Colleges often also sponsor high school diploma programs that run concurrently with their college classes.

**Fear: I could never pass those entrance exams
the colleges make you take.**

And guess what? You won't have to, at least not at your local community college. The SAT (Scholastic Aptitude Test) and ACT (American College Test) are given to high school seniors to compare them with each other and to predict how well they will do in college.

But adult students practically never have to submit these scores to get admitted to a college. The assessment tests colleges give (see Basic Skills above) are usually all that's required.

Fighting the fear of entrance exams

1. You probably won't have to take them, certainly not at a community college.

2. Most four year schools waive the entrance exam requirements for students who are transferring in as Juniors from a community college. A decent GPA is about all you're going to need.

> "The kids made me nervous. A couple of times when I went in they'd say, 'gee, you're my mom's age.' And I said, 'OK, then think of me that way and we'll be fine.' ...But ironically I found that I got along really well with the kids."
>
> *Linda W., 41, started school in her 20s and graduated about 20 years later with a Bachelor's degree. Her GPA was about 3.3.*

Fear: I'm going to be a misfit in that place, surrounded by people young enough to be <u>my</u> kids.

You'll be delighted to learn that most colleges are jam-packed with adult students. About half of everyone in college in this country is over 25. Adult students are all over every campus, and their numbers grow every semester. Most colleges would simply have to close their doors if they lost the financial support that adult students contribute. Still worried? Consider a few points....

Fighting the fear of being the misfit as an adult student
Consider these facts:
1. The average age of a college student is now about 30.
2. About 2/3 of all college students are part-time students.
3. Adult students almost always get better grades than younger students.
4. Adult students often become the leaders in everything from classroom discussions to special campus groups like the student newspaper, social action groups and clubs.
5. Adults students are almost invariably looked up to by the younger students, and these young students often seek adult students out for advice and help. Maybe your kids never listened to you - but you can bet the young kids in your classes will!

> **"I always tell my husband that (the cost of college) is about like buying a used car."**
> *Ann H.*

Fear: I'll never be able to afford college.

While it isn't getting any cheaper to go to school, you'll be pleasantly surprised at how much help is actually available to help pay for your education. There's an entire chapter in this book devoted to financing, but briefly....

Fighting the fear of not having enough money
1. Community colleges in particular are usually <u>much</u> less expensive than four year schools. Taking two years at your community college and transferring into a four year school can save you <u>lots</u> of money.
2. Employers may pick up all or most of the cost of college courses for their employees. Your personnel office or your union will have the details.
3. Most adult students will qualify for some sort of financial aid, from loans and grants to outright scholarships. The financial aid office at your college will give you all the information and forms you need to start the process.
4. There are lots of ways to cut the costs of transportation, meals, books and supplies, all necessary and expensive additions to the cost of basic tuition. See Chapter 7.

> "I got As in both those classes and that's what sort of got me on a roll. Once I saw that I could be successful I thought, Oh, OK, maybe this isn't so bad."
> *Ann H.*

**Fear: I was always nervous taking tests.
I'll never be able to pass them.**

You're already doing fine in the tests that really matter, your daily life as a mate, a parent, an employee and a friend. And while test anxiety is pretty common in students of all ages, there are ways to conquer these natural fears. Try these tips....

Fighting the fear of tests
1. Your local college is very well aware that people get nervous about tests. Many schools run special seminars on exactly this subject, and the results are usually very good. You'll find lots of people of all ages in these seminars: it's not just adults who get jittery about tests.
2. There are many books available on test anxiety. Your school or public library can point you to them.
3. There are ways to take tests that increase your chances of passing them. We've devoted a whole chapter to this subject. See chapter 28.
4. Believe it or not, some classes don't even require tests.
5. Some instructors are very flexible in how they gauge your learning, and might offer to let you do a paper or a project in place of a test.

> "I have a friend and she didn't charge me. And another friend who did charge, but it was very minimal. Mostly it's working the schedules so I didn't have that big expense."
> *Evelyn S. started college with two children. She still has the two kids, but now she also has a Bachelor's Degree and a 3.5 GPA.*

Fear: I have small children and child care is so expensive. How can I go to school with little kids to raise?

Childcare is a major issue in adult education, and there is an entire chapter on that subject in this book. Children unquestionably complicate your life and your plans for school, but they don't eliminate the possibility. You just have to be more creative. Here are some ideas....

Fighting the fear of the child care dilemma
1. More and more schools are devoting resources to dealing with this question, and many offer low cost child care right on the campus. Check with the counseling or admissions office to see what your school has.
2. Students often team up, with one watching all the kids while the other parents go to classes. Then the responsibility rotates, with the first parent taking the duty. Some students actually form clubs of several people.
3. Night and weekend classes can offer more flexibility for the babysitters and students alike.
4. Distance learning classes of all types can allow you to learn at home.

> "Being an older student gives you the opportunity to relax with your professors and see them as human beings."
> *Patrick A., 46 and married with two children, started at his local community college and ultimately earned his Bachelor's Degree.*

Fear: Instructors and students won't like me because I'm too old.

Actually, age is pretty much a non-issue in college, and you are going to be very surprised at how well you get along with your teachers and the younger students. But if you're still concerned because you've got a little gray in your hair, consider these points...

Fighting the fear of being too old for college

1. As noted above, the average college student these days is about 30. And in many, many classes, he or she is a <u>lot</u> over 30.

2. Also as noted above, older students generally get better grades. The reason for that is that they pay closer attention in class, ask more questions and study better: all characteristics that will make you look good to your instructors.

3. You are probably close in age to many of your instructors. And that's good news for both of you. You'll find you have a lot in common with those teachers, much more than the young kids do. Will all those common experiences help you in class? What do you think?

4. Older students always bring their wealth of living experiences into the classroom, and the younger students in particular love that.

> *"If I see an hour laying around, I pick it up, tuck it away for later."*
> *Patrick A., 46, on time management skills.*

Fear: I don't have the time to go to college.

While this might actually seem true at first glance, it's usually the very busy people who do find the time. The adult students who were interviewed for this book were all very busy, and they still found the time to go to school. So have the many hundreds of students I have advised over the years. They all did it by managing their time effectively. See Chapter 11 for more information on this topic.

And you don't have to completely give up the rest of your life to make time for college...you merely have to rearrange it a bit. Try these tactics:

Fighting the fear of not having enough time
1. Most colleges offer courses on different schedules to accommodate busy people like you - one or two nights a week, weekends, early in the morning, during lunch hours, short accelerated courses in the summer and between long semesters, etc.
2. Employers can often be very flexible for employees who are trying to better themselves. It can't hurt to ask if they will modify your work schedule somewhat to suit your college schedule needs.
3. Online courses don't even require you to be in a classroom - you can do much of the work at home, on your own schedule.
4. Consider a shorter program. Maybe your goal can be an Associate's degree or a Certificate for now.

Fear: I'll outgrow my friends and mate if I go to college.

This is a very real possibility, and anyone who tells you otherwise is kidding you. Education makes us grow and expands our horizons and interests. Education changes the people who get it, that's a fact. Consider these possibilities to avoid this problem:

Fighting the fear that you'll outgrow those around you
1. Your mate may want to go to school themselves and just never mentioned it because <u>they</u> were afraid of outgrowing <u>you</u>. Talk to them about it. You might be surprised at the result.
2. Education is transparent to really good friends. Solid friendships have usually been that way for years, and should be able to weather the change.
3. Try to involve your friends and family in school-related activities. Most instructors will allow guests in their classrooms, and all colleges run a wide variety of activities on campus that you can take friends and family to - plays, movies, concerts, readings, sports events, etc.

Fear: I don't have a college anywhere near me.

And you don't really need one these days. In the not-too-distant past you had to sit in a classroom to be a learner. Not anymore. Here's why....

Fighting the fear of distance
1. The term Distance Learning is just what it implies. Almost all schools offer a variety of courses that are based outside the classroom. Possibilities include the Internet, correspondence courses, televised courses, videotaped courses and the ability to simply test out of courses. Chapters 16 and 17 provide some additional details.

> **"As I walked around campus I saw a lot of older people. You know, my age, and older or younger, but in their 30s and 40s and 50s. You feel a little bit better, a little more at home."**
> *Deanne L., 39 and the mother of two kids, started school at a community college in her early 20s. She kept at it a bit at a time and earned a Bachelor's Degree in her 40s.*

CHAPTER 4

Getting Yourself Organized and Finding The Support You Need

> "My schedule is just filled, from the minute I get up, between studying and work and trying to have some kind of life in-between."
>
> *Lorene K., 41, worked more than 40 hours a week as a waitress and carried a fulltime course load. She earned her Associate's degree in 1999 and her Bachelor's a couple of years later.*

Get Organized!

If you've always been the sort of person who required other people to pick up after you, had trouble getting places on time, or whose life always seemed to be generally in a shambles, beware: college is going to require massive amounts of personal organizational skill. If you don't already have it, or don't think you can develop it, you may want to reconsider your decision to pursue a degree.

It's still possible to go to school, of course. But it won't be possible to crash through the project at a very high rate. You may have to limit yourself to a course here, a course there.

And while there's certainly nothing wrong with that approach, someone who is very well organized will be able to complete their degree in relatively short order. Even if they are working full time, are in a relationship, have kids, and assume all the other assorted responsibilities that adults typically have.

The whole key to getting your degree in a fairly short period of time is organization, both in your personal life and in your work life. Most of us only get 24 hour days, and we have to figure out what we're going to use those hours for. So going to college while trying to maintain the other parts of your life at something like normal levels is basically a time management problem. Let's look at the two areas of your life that use most of your time.

Organize your personal life

The people around you, your partner, your kids, your parents, even your neighbors and friends, all will have an effect on your ability to go to college. If you are constantly involved in doing things for other people, you will never be able to set aside the large chunks of time required to get a degree.

And that's really what this section is all about: time. There is a whole chapter devoted to that topic later in this book, but for now let's examine it briefly.

There is only so much time in a given day or week or year. Some of that time is already spoken for. Your employer wants some, typically 40 hours a week, about 50 weeks per year. (Anyone working much more than that for extended periods is going to have a much harder time fitting college into their schedule.) That work time is gone. Six or eight hours a day is going to be allocated to sleeping, and while you may be able to get away with less every now and then, most of us require that extended nap every night. Kiss that time goodbye too. The best you can hope for there is pleasant dreams.

The time you are left with is roughly eight hours a day from Monday to Friday, and perhaps 16 hours a day on Saturday and Sunday and holidays and vacations. From that time you must subtract your part of the responsibility for all of the other things that adults/partners/parents have to do just to stay alive and keep the household running.

Someone in your family has to go shopping, run errands, cook meals, cut the grass, shovel the snow (if you're in the north), maybe take the kids to school, attend plays and PTA conferences, put gas in the car, go to the dry cleaners, do the banking and on and on and on. Unless you are one of those unique individuals who has figured out how to be in two places at once, or who has discovered the secret of time travel, all of these little chores describe your daily life.

And those little chores chew up time. A lot of time. And if you allow them to occupy most of that "spare" time during the week and on the weekends, you will never have the time required to go to school.

Many beginning adult students get discouraged early on because they find that they no longer have the time to do all of the things that they used to do. You have to be prepared to sacrifice your involvement in a lot of those activities. Sometimes that's not a problem, because you never really wanted to take care of the dry cleaning or cut the grass anyway, and going to school gives you a convenient excuse to pass that chore on to someone else.

Chores are one thing, and many of us really don't want to do them anyway. But in many cases you are going to find that you also cannot do a lot of the pleasurable things you used to do.

You won't be able to make all the parent-teacher conferences or see all the school plays. You won't have time to putter around in the garden for hours every week. You won't be able to go to the movies every weekend or watch the games with your friends or spend hours on your hobby, whatever it is.

If you aren't prepared to make these sorts of sacrifices, you will never find the time necessary to go to school. It's that simple.

> "I just prioritize. I put school first. School and my kids are right there at the top. And then work is third. And I just work everything around my school schedule."
> *Jason B, 27, has four kids, two jobs and a full-time course load. Along with a 3.56 GPA.*

Family support is absolutely crucial

Once you've decided that you are prepared to make the necessary adjustments in your life, your very first step should be talking with your family about the importance of getting your degree. Because they will be required to make a lot of adjustments as well.

Start by discussing your plans with your spouse or partner. Although you can fill in the exact details later, you need to have the broad outlines already in place if this conversation is going to be productive.

This is especially true if your partner has no inkling that you are considering returning to college. You need to be able to explain what you are planning to do: where you will be attending college, about how many hours a week you'll be in class or in transit to and from school or doing homework, how many classes you'll be taking, what your new schedule will look like, how college is going to be paid for, and - if you have small kids - what the day care situation looks like if that's going to be an issue.

Most importantly, you must be able to <u>justify</u> this huge change in the way your family functions:

- <u>Why</u> do you want to return to school and get your degree?
- <u>What</u> do you think it is going to do for you? For your family?
- <u>How</u> <u>long</u> is it going to take?
- Is it <u>worth</u> the time, the money, the effort, the confusion, the change that it is going to create? Why?
- What makes you think you can actually do this?

Your spouse or partner has every right in the world to ask you these questions. You need to have the answers.

This book and others like it can provide general guidance and direction, but every person is different. Only you can give specific answers to questions like those. So before you begin discussion of this important topic with your significant other and the rest of your family, you need to spend some time thinking about what this proposed change will do to you and your family and the relationships among all the people in your family. The eventual plusses need to outweigh the short-term minuses if this is going to work.

Once you enlist the support of your mate, you should assemble the rest of the family and tell them what you are planning to do. The same arguments you used to convince your partner can be used here. But at this point in the process you presumably have your partner on your side, and they can help explain what's going on to the rest of the family.

But remember that children do not enjoy the ability to take the long view. The child's life is very 'now' oriented. For a small child, even the concept of this afternoon or this evening is alien: they simply don't understand the passage of time. The older they get the more they understand this, but they will be teenagers before they truly have much of a grasp of the future, and even then it won't be as good as yours.

> "To be honest, I just couldn't make it without their support. Does it cause conflict? No, not any more. At first it did, because it was a change. Mom was doing something different, Bette was doing something different. And all of a sudden, instead of having just three people in my life, I had three people plus a lot of books."
>
> *Bette B, married and the mother of two teenagers, started school when she was 39. She earned her Associate's degree in 1999 and ultimately expects to get a Master's. Her 4.0 GPA is a good indication that she will.*

Younger children in particular will need to be reassured that you will still be there for them when they need you, and you will need to develop a plan that will allow you to do this. The chapters on Time Management and Studying will give you some ideas, but the plan will have to come from you.

Remember that you won't be the only one who will be going through changes here. The rest of your family will be too. Your time will be much more scheduled, and there will be things that you will just not be able to do for them anymore. To the best of their ages and abilities, the kids will need to understand this. And they will need to be behind you in your decision.

If you are in the category of people who has to have a degree to move up in your company or profession, your degree is going to have a lot of monetary significance. In the previous chapter we saw that a Bachelor's degree has the potential to add many thousands of dollars a year to your income. Over your working life, the difference between having a degree and not having one can add up to many hundreds of thousands of dollars in extra income. Your partner and your children need to understand this and support your goal. If anyone in your immediate family is against your going back to school, it will be much harder to do it. They must support you 110%.

> **"The kids are great. They're planning this big party for me the day before graduation."**
> *Kathleen C.'s children are all adults now, but they've been watching her go to school off and on for nearly three decades.*

Even your parents, friends and neighbors should be supportive. Sooner or later you are going to need a little unscheduled help - emergency babysitting, a ride to school or the library because your car is in the shop, etc. You can never have too much support.

Moral support and time:
You can never have enough of either

You are looking for two things here: moral support and extra time. If your life is completely consumed waiting on others to fulfill their needs, you will never be able to find the time and energy to go to school. You must be able to depend on the others around you to pick up many of the responsibilities you used to shoulder. Once you are in college and start classes, you will not have the time to continue to do most of the shopping or take care of getting the car washed or spend hours each week doing lawn maintenance, laundry, house cleaning, etc.

Bette Talks about family support

"We sat down one night, it was in March of my first semester that I came back to school. And I said, I can't make it anymore, I can't take it. I'm going to quit school because I can't do everything by myself.

I was doing the dishes, I was doing the total upkeep of the house, I was taking care of everything that everybody needed, plus what I was doing. It wasn't going anywhere. I wasn't getting any help.

But it all changed after that little family meeting. They all of a sudden realized that mom needs us too, or the wife needs me. And they work with me very well now. My boys know how to vacuum, they know how to cook. We all help each other out."

Bette was nearly 40 when she started college.

You should try to determine what things need to be done, how much time they take, who is doing them now, and whether they are really necessary. Do you really need to cut the grass every week? Maybe you can scale this chore back to every ten days and no one will be the wiser. Over time that may save you several hours a month. And that simple change might be enough time to do the required reading for half of a course. If you could just assign this chore to your partner or one of the older kids, you wouldn't have to do it at all. And that's probably enough time to do the required reading for the entire course.

Can you combine errands so that they take less total time? Think creatively about all of the tasks that go into keeping a household running, and then try to allocate those chores so that other household members do more of them and you do fewer. Every chore that gets cut back in time or reassigned to someone else means more time for you.

And you are going to need every minute you can get your hands on.

> **Ann talks about time management**
>
> "You can't spread yourself too thin and make a hundred promises to a hundred people. Sometimes you just gotta say, hey! Christmas dinner is sandwiches this year! You can't kill yourself and try to be perfect.
> Because I've tried to be perfect once in awhile and it's like, nah! Forget it! The house is dirty, the lawn is tall, there's snow in the driveway. You get over it. The neighbors might not, but you do."

Ann was 33 and the mother of one child when she started school. She earned her BA and continued on in a Master's program.

Organize your work life

Although an occasional adult student is able to work 50 or 60 or more hours a week and still take a fairly heavy college course load, those folks are rare. And most of them tend to toast themselves pretty quickly. By the end of a semester or two their employment and/or their college work begins to suffer. They are forced to cut back on something. So if you're used to devoting large amounts of time to your job, and you're not ready to cut those hours back, you will probably have to re-think the amount of time you can spend on school. You'll still be able to squeeze in a course here or there.

But that's about it. You are never going to have the time required to blow through a degree in much less than a decade. There are just not that many hours in a day, and you will have already used most of them in the service of your employer.

If you are working a more normal schedule of 40 or so hours a week, there is enough time potentially available to go to school. Millions of people are already doing it, and you can too. All it takes is organization.

So why do you need to organize your work life? Simply because - like your family - your employer has the ability to use your precious time. And that drain on your time can interfere with your class and study schedule.

Talk with your manager as soon as you've made the decision to go back to school. You should probably try to have some rationale for going to college that will help your company in the long run. If you can show your manager some benefits, you will make it a lot easier for him or her to cut you some slack every now and then. Courses leading to a degree that is usable in your company are of obvious value, of course, but even general college-level training can certainly have some benefit to your employer.

Although every employee is different, most employers realize that better-educated people make better employees. A study by the University of Pennsylvania, quoted in the March/April 1997 issue of Adult Learning (*The New Workplace and Lifelong Learning* by Robert Jones), notes that companies who increased the educational level of their work force by one year saw an 8.6 percent increase in productivity. Most companies understand that their biggest asset is people, and that these people have a direct, critical impact on the quality of their products and services. With the strongly competitive business environment of today's world, most employers should have no trouble seeing the value in more education for you.

You can only hope this is true where you work, because you are going to need as much support from your employer as you can get. He can either be a tremendous help to you on the college front or a tremendous hindrance. If you are constantly at odds with your manager over your other responsibilities outside of the office or the plant, you are going to have a lot of trouble convincing him or her that taking on even more responsibility by going to school is a good idea. You need full support for this project from your boss.

> **"And I let my employer know that a new semester is getting ready to start, my schedule is going to be changing. And fortunately they're really flexible with me and they've been able to work around my schedule. ....It's made it a lot easier."**
> *Jason B., 27 and the father of four, worked a full time job and a part-time job. He received his Associate's degree in the late 90s and is on the way to an eventual Master's.*

There is no way to predict precisely what sort of cooperation you may end up needing from your employer over the course of five or more years in school. But I can give you a few examples from my own experience that will illustrate how a cooperative manager and company can be of great help to you.

Mike Doolin

One semester toward the end of my long college career I needed to take two courses that were never offered at night. (This was just poor planning on my part, and should not have happened, but it did.) One class was held at 8 AM, the other around 2 PM. The college I was attending was 75 miles away. I got my manager to agree to let me take my vacation <u>one hour</u> at a time. This let me drive to the early class, take it, drive back to work for a few hours, then drive back to the school for the 2 PM class. There would have been no way to accommodate those classes without this flexibility.

My employer always looked the other way when I needed to make a few photocopies of something for a class. You will certainly run into many situations where you need copies of something - a paper, a piece of research, some pages from a text - something. Unless you already own a copier, you will have to go to a commercial copy store or your school's library and pay them for the privilege. And chew up valuable time in the process.

I was scheduled to go out of town once to set up and attend a trade show from Saturday to Saturday. I had an important test scheduled in a class on a Monday that I would have missed. My employer found someone else to set the show up and graciously allowed me to fly in on Tuesday morning.

I managed to get through several courses by doing a project instead of attending classes. For a couple of these the project I did was intimately related to the work I was doing for my employer. He didn't have to allow me to take these confidential materials out of the building and show them to my professors to get credit for them. But he did.

You may also be able to buy the school supplies or computer equipment you need through your employer, and hitchhike on his greater purchasing power for those pens and pencils and printer cartridges and the occasional complete computer system you're going to need. It probably won't save you a fortune, but a few bucks here and there can add up.

Organizing your work life also means being able to look as far ahead as possible in your work responsibilities and meshing them into your class schedule. Maybe your employer will allow you to work a few less hours during this class semester in exchange for a few more during your busy work season. If you schedule your classes carefully - perhaps by taking one more this semester and one less the next - your total hours between school and work won't change much. Maybe he'll allow you access to your company's computer systems to do papers and other projects on during your lunch hour or on breaks. Maybe he'll let you work at home one or two days a week, saving you the time necessary to commute. Tactics like these give you the flexibility you need to keep working on that degree at a steady pace.

It's also possible that you currently work for an employer who is just not very understanding of your desire to go to college and isn't willing to give you the amount of cooperation you'll need. If you are unfortunate enough to be in this position, you may find that you need to change employers to pursue your degree.

> "So I went to my boss and asked her if it was possible for me to rearrange my schedule. I'd still put in 40 hours, because of the four of us working there, I was the only one who was there eight to five. Everyone else was a part-timer. And she said, no, it's a choice between your job and your education."
> Kathleen C., 56 and a grandmother, finished her Bachelor's degree in the late 1990s. She started college in 1971.

A note or two to conclude this chapter. If you have a reputation as a difficult employee, one who is always grumbling about work conditions and the relative stupidity of your management, one who is hard to get along with, one who never wants to do more than the bare minimum required, you are going to have a very hard time getting much cooperation out of your company. They have watched you be a pain for all this time, and now that you want something from them, they will probably just laugh at your requests.

Don't be surprised. What goes around comes around. Conversely, if you have always been a helpful, cooperative employee, your work has always been good and you're not a troublemaker, you will probably find your management willing to help you out. You had better hope that they will be cooperative, because you are going to need all the help you can get.

> **"It's very important, especially if you're...married,.... that each partner understands what the other is going through."**
>
> *Dave P., 49, beat cancer and decided to go back to college. He finished his Bachelor's degree in June 1998 and is now working on his Ph.D.*

CHAPTER 5

How Fast Can You Actually Get A Degree?

> "Four years ago I said: 'In four years I can say I'm gonna be done in a minute,' or 'I really should have started then.' "
>
> *Patrick A., 46, married and the father of two kids, managed to work 20+ hours a week and go to school nearly full time.*

The average college education is only about 40 courses

That's approximately 120 credit hours. These are rough numbers - every school is a bit different. But for our purposes they are close enough. Let's do a little math.

If you could attend college full time the way the kids do, you would take about ten courses/30 hours per year. Most of the 18 through 21 year-old crowd put in two semesters - Fall and Spring - and take the summers off. That works fine for them. But that lackadaisical attitude is not going to help you much. You're a real grownup now, and you know how to hustle better than the kids.

Many schools run year round. There are two common schedules: semesters and quarters.

The semester system

A typical college on the semester system has a 15 or 16 week Fall semester running from early September to Christmas, another 15 or 16 week Spring (sometimes called Winter) semester running from sometime in January to the end of April or early May, then two shorter Summer semesters, each about 6 or so weeks long. These short sessions run from May through June, and from July through August. Some schools also have what are called Intersessions, which are two to three week crash sessions which run between the longer Fall and Winter/Spring semesters.

The quarter system

Other schools run on the quarter system, which provides four course periods of roughly equal length, usually around 10 or 11 weeks per quarter. Schools on the quarter system usually require about 180 credit hours to graduate, but the courses are 4 or 5 credit hours instead of 3. It still works out to about 40 courses total.

School schedules are flexible

The point here is that there is usually a selection of times available to take a course. You don't have to limit yourself to the long Fall or Winter/Spring semesters, or even to just certain periods of the year. Most schools' schedules will accommodate you year round in some fashion or another.

Let's go back to the math. If a typical degree is just 40 courses, and you decide you want to get through it in, say, six years, that's only 6.66 courses per year...call it seven courses. Spaced over a full year, that could work out to a schedule like this:

Example A:
A typical 12 month class schedule:

Fall:	2 classes x 3 hours = 6 hours
Intersession:	1 class x 3 hours = 3 hours = 9 hours total earned
Spring:	3 classes x 3 hours = 9 hours = 18 hours total earned
Summer I & II:	2 classes x 3 hours = 6 hours = 24 hours total earned

Example B:
An alternate schedule:

Fall:	3 classes x 3 hours = 9 hours
Intersession:	off
Spring:	3 classes x 3 hours = 9 hours = 18 hours total earned
Summer I:	2 classes x 3 hours = 6 hours = 24 hours total earned

In both these examples you are racking up hours nearly as fast as a full time day student. In a year you would have earned 24 hours, vs about 30 that a full time day school student would have earned. Not too bad for someone with a lot of other responsibilities! Let's look at both of these briefly.

Realistically, Example A would be a very tough schedule to stay on for any length of time for those of us who have other things to do beside go to school, particularly if all of these credits had to be earned in a classroom setting. (There are a lot of other ways to get credit, and we'll talk about them later in Chapters 16 and 17). This schedule keeps you busy with schoolwork 12 months out of the year. And while it's balanced in terms of actual work load, it never gives you a break - there's always another test, another assignment, another class. And it makes it very difficult to schedule longer family events like vacations. And because you are never completely free of school responsibilities, it is equally hard to devote much time to family and household chores of any length.

> "I took a couple of courses a semester, right from the time I was 21 until I was pregnant with my first child when I was 27. Then I took six years off while my kids were little."
> *Valerie G., 38, started college in 1977. She finished her Bachelor's degree in the late 1990s and went to work on a Master's. She expects to earn a Doctorate eventually.*

Example B, with three classes in each of the long semesters, is certainly a bit more frantic in terms of schoolwork. You would be <u>very</u> busy on this schedule. But you would only be very busy for about 15 or 16 weeks, and then you would get a little break. Even attending the Fall-Spring semesters back-to-back, you would never be in school longer than about 5 months at a stretch, and then you would get some time off. This schedule puts you back into the first Summer school session almost immediately after the end of the Spring semester in May, but only for about 5 or 6 weeks, then gives you the rest of the summer free. You also get the 3 or 4 week break that is typical of the space between the Fall and Spring semesters.

The point of this little exercise is to demonstrate that if your school runs year round - and nearly all of them do these days - you have the opportunity to earn a fair amount of hours in a reasonable amount of time just by carefully scheduling classes. The trick is to just keep grinding away at it, a course or two at a time.

And you don't necessarily have to attend every session. If you are willing to work pretty hard for short bursts of a few months, this system allows you to accumulate credit at a very respectable rate without completely toasting yourself. And this example only uses the more conventional, classroom-based way to earn credit. There are lots of other techniques, and many of them don't require regular schedules like these.

> **"I carry books all the time, because I never know when I'm going to get that free moment."**
> *Jason B. worked a full time job, a part time job and carried a full time class load. He earned his Associate's and went on for his Bachelor's.*

Some classes, of course, will be four hours or two hours, not three. But on average it should be possible to earn somewhere around 20 hours/7 courses per year, which puts you on a respectable six year schedule to earn your four year degree.

Completing one extra class in every year - eight classes instead of seven - will cut a full year off the project, enabling you to get through in five years, not six. While that's a pretty heavy load for a part time working student to actually attend classes, it can certainly be done.

If it's any consolation, a year 2000 study by the Graduate School of Education and Information at the University of California at Los Angeles that tracked 56,818 students who entered 262 four-year colleges and universities in the fall semester of 1994 (http://www.gseis.ucla.edu/heri/darcu_pr.html) shows that only about 36% of graduates completed a Bachelor's degree in four years. This study also shows that about 59% of people manage to get through in six years or less.

The US Census Condition of Education 2004 study referenced earlier (http://nces.ed.gov/pubs2004/2004077.pdf) comes to very similar conclusions, and shows that only about 55% of the people originally enrolled in a four year school have earned a Bachelor's degree at the end of five years.

So you have nothing to feel embarrassed about if it takes you six years or even longer. Even though you probably will feel some pressure to complete your degree quickly, it's not a race. Better to go a bit slower and do a little better.

The point of this short exercise is to get you used to thinking in terms of courses and hours, and how those translate into years of your life.

Is there a way to cut this time to degree completion down? Yes. A number of ways. And we'll cover them in later chapters. Some of the smarter day-school students have used these techniques to cut their transit time down to three years or less, and you can do the same thing.

> "I like the Saturday 8 AM to 4 PM courses because you can get a whole course into 5 or 6 weeks. Even though it makes for a long day, it's over in a month, month and a half. And I don't feel bored with the subject."
> *Kevin R., 34, married with two children, finished his Bachelor's Degree in about 10 years.*

CHAPTER 6

What Kind Of A Degree Do You Really Need?

> "I told my supervisor I wanted to go back to school, and he said, for what? And I said, Art. And he said, no, we won't pay for that."
> *Helen D., 40 and a single mom, got her Bachelor's degree in Art. Her employer eventually reconsidered, and paid her tuition.*

No one really cares what kind of degree you have

Once you get your degree and start moving as an equal through the world of other folks who have also graduated from college, you'll be continually amazed at something that never occurred to me when I was still working on my Bachelor's. It's this: almost no one <u>cares</u> about what kind of a Bachelor's degree you have!

What?! After all those years, all that hard work, all that personal and emotional strain on both you and your family?! All those books and tests and papers! All those closed libraries and parking tickets and thankless assignments! All that careful planning and jockeying and hours spent with course catalogs trying to make sure you took the right courses at the right time? And all that money you spent!

And no one cares what your degree is in??!!

No, they really don't.

But that statement obviously deserves some qualification. There are many jobs that require a certain kind of degree and nothing else will do. Some professions like medicine and law and accounting and engineering and science and teaching require you to have very specific academic qualifications. If you want to enter one of these professions you will have to pursue a very rigid series of courses. Credentials here are more than just important - they are absolutely crucial. There are few if any shortcuts allowed.

But for the rest of us - and that's many millions of people - well, we're generalists for the most part. We work in offices and factories and plants, in marketing and customer relations or quality control or shipping. We work in government or the military or run small retail locations or own our own businesses.

And guess what? Most of these organizations just do not care what your major is in. For the most part they will allow you to work in pretty much any capacity you want, as long as you can convince them of two things:

1. You graduated from college;
2. You are interested in their company and the position you are applying for.

Countless people in their 30s, 40s, 50s, 60s and beyond have degrees that have absolutely no bearing whatsoever on their current jobs. My plumber has a Master's degree in psychology. A good friend of mine runs a screenprinting equipment company where he designs a lot of very sophisticated mechanical and electrical equipment. His degree is in sociology. Until very recently my wife was head of sales in a fast growing advertising agency. She has a Master's in English. What do these degrees have to do with the work these people are performing?

> **"The world is rigged for higher education. I sure didn't want to be an adult student. (But) I just didn't want to be a 60-year old flipping burgers....and taking orders from some 21-year old."**
> *Kevin R., 34, married and the father of two children, is an RN who changed careers. He earned his Bachelor's in the late 1990s and continued on for his Master's.*

In general, not much. For these folks and millions more, a college education only opened the door. It didn't specifically prepare them for a particular job or career. They got and kept the job and career they are in because they knew how to learn, worked hard, were interested in what they were doing, and had a good attitude.

Their degrees didn't have much at all to do with their success. It only got them in the door, past the sign that said "Only people with college educations need apply." And that is really what you want a degree for: to get into that short line, to get pre-qualified for all those millions of jobs that simply say: 'college degree required.'

Why don't most jobs require specific degrees? I have a theory about that. Here it is: About half of the courses in every Bachelor's degree program are pretty much the same from major to major, no matter what your major is. The liberal arts folks, engineers, psychologists, sociologists, pre-med, pre-law and business students all take virtually identical courses for about their first two years of school.

Remember this - it will become important in later discussions.

No matter what field you are going into, no matter where you go to school, there are certain basic courses that you will have to take. These core courses are in the Humanities, the Social Sciences, the Natural Sciences and Mathematics, and usually include courses in Writing, Intro to English Literature, History, Basic Math, a beginning Science like Physics, Biology, Geology or Chemistry, Psychology, Sociology, Phys Ed and a few others. Everyone - <u>everyone</u> - takes these classes. So about half of everyone's Bachelor's degree is virtually identical. And everyone knows that.

What that Bachelor's degree really means
Most employers just do not care very much about <u>what</u> your degree is in. They are much more interested in the fact that you <u>have</u> a degree, any degree. That college degree demonstrates that you know how to learn, that you can set and meet goals and that you can assume responsibility. It shows that you have developed the critical thinking skills necessary to view situations in a problem-solution manner and do the required research to solve the problem.

In short, it demonstrates that you are now an educated adult. It is the <u>process</u> of gaining an education that is important to most employers, not the specific end product of that education.

Since that is generally true (with the exceptions noted above), you can use this information for your benefit when you are designing your own college program.

> "Even if you don't change jobs or you don't change careers, learning can never be bad. .... nothing you ever learn will go to waste."
> *Evelyn S., 41 and the married mother of two children, became disabled on the job and retrained to become a grammar school teacher.*

A few hints: Unless you are targeting a specific career like law, medicine, engineering, accounting and a few others, your fastest route through a college education is probably a generalized, liberal arts degree. Most of the courses in a Liberal Arts program are interesting, and you will probably find a great many courses that you are attracted to. Liberal Arts curricula give you a lot of flexibility in determining which courses to take. And that flexibility can speed up your trip to a degree.

Another hint: If you are already working in a particular discipline, try to major in that. Why? Because your on-the-job training gives you a head start in at least some of the courses you will have to take. And because you may be able to use the knowledge you have already gained in your job to avoid having to sit through certain classes to get credit. More on that topic in Chapters 16 and 17, where we discuss a number of techniques that can chop a lot of time off your college career.

Bottom line: You can probably make your trip through college somewhat faster and simpler by taking courses that are either A) easier and probably more interesting than some others and/or B) on a subject you already know something about.

> "People who found it difficult to imagine when they arrived here that they really can get the BA are now looking at further education in ways that they would have found incomprehensible. Certainly they couldn't have imagined this when they first approached us."
> *Sharon Grigsby recruits adult students for SUNY Empire State College, one of the very first non-traditional, non-residential colleges in the country.*

CHAPTER 7

Who's Paying For All This? How To Find The $$$!

> "Ultimately, I'm the one who made the choice. I'm the one who's paying the bills, I'm the one who put my name on the loans. And if I miss something, I'm the one who has to take the hit. I don't have to apologize to the professor, I don't have to make excuses. I just say OK, I'll make this up. I'll recover."
>
> *Patrick A., 46, married and the father of two children, cut back from a full time job to a part time one and decided to attend college nearly full time. It took him about 5 years.*

Hang onto your wallet
This could be an expensive trip

If you are one of those rare individuals who can afford to pay for his or her complete college education, you don't even need to read this chapter. Just go to the college of your choice and whip out your checkbook. They will be delighted to see you.

Most of us, however, will get a serious case of sticker shock when we check a few college catalogs for pricing information. College is expensive. College can be very expensive. Next to your house or a luxury car, a college education will probably be the most expensive thing you will ever buy. (Unlike those things, however, it will continue to pay dividends for the rest of your life.)

One of the recognized authorities - the College Board – (http://www.collegeboard.com/article/0,3868,6-29-0-4494,00.html) estimates that the average yearly cost of a four year education in a public college or university for 2005-2006 is about $5491. The same education at a private school is going to set you back about $21,235, on average. The College Board notes, however, that about 60% of students attending public four-year schools pay less than $6000/year.

With prices like these, it makes very good sense to sit down early on in the process and figure out where the money is coming from and where it's going. Because it will be going.

We'll talk about detailed budgeting later, in Chapter 10, but for now you should just do some rough estimating on costs and conduct some research to see if you are eligible for any sort of financial help from any source.

Most of the students interviewed for this book, and the many thousands of students I have advised over the years, received some type of financial help, in the form of loans, grants, scholarships, work-study opportunities or employer assistance. In the article referenced above, the College Board notes that about 60% of students receive grant aid.

Who might help? There are a lot more places to get financial help than you might imagine. This list is not intended to be exhaustive, but it is pretty complete:

Your employer

Start your research where you work. Many corporations have a tuition assistance program that might pick up some or even all of your college costs. Some programs cover just tuition, while others also pay for books (which can be very pricey) and fees such as lab fees, student activity fees, parking permits, etc.

> "I was in Industrial Relations and the manager said, I didn't know you were going to school, I didn't see any tuition aid forms coming through. And I said, well, my manager told me the company wouldn't pay for it because it's an Art degree. And he said, as long as it's a matriculated program, we'll pay for it."
>
> *Helen D., 40 and a single mother, paid for the first two years of her degree out of her own pocket until this chance conversation got her into the tuition reimbursement program at her company.*

Many company reimbursement programs require you to prepay the tuition or other covered expense, take the course, then turn in a grade report showing some minimum level of performance, usually a C or better. Then you get some portion of your tuition (and/or books and/or fees) back from your employer.

If you are one of the lucky ones whose employer covers your educational expenses 100%, and you stay on the same course load schedule semester after semester, you only have to front the money your first semester and keep your grades up. From that point on you can just use your reimbursement check from the previous semester to cover the next semester's costs.

Some schools have a system that lets you defer payment of tuition until the end of the semester if they know that your company will be reimbursing you, and they may even bill your employer directly. Your Registration or Bursar's office at school or your Personnel office at work will know if your company has a policy of doing this.

Some companies require you to be an employee for a certain length of time before you are eligible for a tuition reimbursement plan, or to take a certain number of credits. Others will only reimburse you for classes which they define as being pertinent to your work and which they approve in advance. Check this out with your personnel department. They have all the details.

If you can't get much info from your in-house people, check the company's web site. There might be more information there. This is particularly important if you are working in a retail location of a large national or multi-national company. Your on-site manager may just not be familiar with the parent company's policies on tuition reimbursement. I have actually personally seen this happen and I have helped a number of students in advising sessions track down the exact web page to show their manager.

What if my company doesn't have a tuition reimbursement policy?

Maybe it's because no one ever asked them to set one up. Or maybe - as in Helen's case noted in the quote above - your immediate manager just doesn't know about the program, or has some details wrong.

If your company truly does not have a reimbursement program, you may be able to get them to institute one. If you have a good relationship with your manager, and you can make a convincing argument that your education (and the education of other co-workers) is going to further the goals of the corporation, you might be able to get them to start a program with your manager's help. It can't hurt to ask.

However, you should be aware that programs like these have a reputation for training people who are going to leave the company once they graduate. With more and more companies looking for ways to cut costs, it may be difficult to convince them to spend more money on a program like this. Still, all they can say is no.

Where else can I go for financial help?
There are a lot of possible sources of financial assistance. Here are a few ideas to get you started.

Your Union: Are you a member of a union? Ask your representative if it offers any sort of help. If it doesn't, ask why not. You might be able to get a program started.

Vets: Are you a military veteran? There is still GI Bill money available in one form or another for a lot of vets, and people who are now in the Armed forces have available programs which are quite generous in exchange for a modest contribution by the service member. The information on www.Military.com/education is very extensive and regularly updated. Check there first.

There are also scholarships available in some states for vets. Call the local Veteran's Administration office to see if you qualify. Also see the Reference section for some useful addresses and phone numbers. This section also includes a listing of the "official" start and end dates of various conflicts the United States has been involved in. If you were on active duty during any of these periods, you may have some special benefits coming to you.

There is also a very good probability that your college has a Veteran's adviser. Check with him or her to see what government benefits might be available for you.

Veteran's Organizations: Your town probably has one or more active vet's groups....Vietnam Vets, American Legion, Veteran's of Foreign Wars, etc. There may be scholarship or grant money available from one of them if you are either a vet or the child of a vet. Check your Yellow pages under Veteran's Organizations, Associations, Clubs, etc.

Military Reservists: Are you in the military reserves? Ask your commanding officer or company/unit clerk or yeoman if you qualify for tuition assistance under any government program.

Child of a deceased or disabled veteran: Some states have special programs available to you.

Disabled Individuals: Both the Federal government and most states have programs to train or re-train people with various disabilities. These programs will often pay for most or all of your expenses, and may even include other items such as computers, books, supplies and fees. Check with your physician, your physical therapist, the campus disabilities office or your college financial aid office.

> **"I have a monthly payment plan. I made a down payment, then every month for four months I make a payment. It's great for an adult student."**
> *Bette B., 40, put in 23 hours a week as an Aide in her school's work/study program to help pay for her college.*

Native Americans: The Bureau of Indian Affairs (BIA) in the U.S. Department of the Interior administers programs that provide financial assistance to enrolled members of tribes, bands or groups recognized by the BIA. Go to http://www.doi.gov/bureau-indian-affairs.html for more information.

Member of any other special identifiable group: There are scholarships and grants available for a mind-boggling array of people. Are you a left-handed ice-skating great-great granddaughter of a Civil War officer? The nephew of a second-cousin who once grew coffee in South America? A third-generation Swede?

These are whimsical examples, of course, but the fact is that millions of dollars in scholarship money for individuals in special classifications goes unclaimed every year simply because no one ever asked for it.

Foundations, religious groups, fraternal organizations, clubs and civic groups, local governments and community groups all may sponsor grants and scholarships. As a start, check with organizations like the American Legion, Kiwanis, Jaycees, YMCA/YWCA, Chamber of Commerce, Girl and Boy Scouts, 4-H Club, American Medical Association, American Bar Association, etc. Sometimes the criteria is as simple as merely living in a given geographic area.

Your library has a lot of reference books listing various types of college scholarships and the criteria you need to meet to apply for them. Your college financial aid office can help here too, and may have more current information than your library. The College Board is a good source of information as well – and they estimate that $129 billion in aid was available for the 2005-2006 college year.

AmeriCorps Program: This Federal program provides full-time educational awards that can be used to either pay for your school as you go or to repay federal student loans. This program puts people to work in community service, before, during or after college. Check their web site at http://www.americorps.org/ for more information.

> **"My grants covered 80 to 90%, and then I would just write a check for the rest."**
> *Dave P., 49 and working full time, started college the first time in 1967. He earned his Bachelor's degree in the late 1990s and expects to continue on to his Ph.D.*

Do you meet financial aid criteria? Your school, state and Federal government will probably all have somewhat different standards for determining your need. Your best source of information here is your college financial aid office.

Here is a list of common <u>Federal</u> tuition aid programs. Be aware that your state and school also have a selection of programs, and you should investigate those as well. And note that although the Federal FAFSA (Free Application for Federal Student Aid) form is the most common way for funding organizations to collect information about you, both your state and your school may well require that you fill out an additional form.

Federal Student Financial Assistance Programs

Aid Program	Eligibility	Amount Available	How to Apply
Pell Grant	US citizen or permanent resident who is matriculated and enrolled for 3 credits or more. Students must not have a BA degree, be in default on a student loan or owe a refund of federal aid funds.	Up to a yearly maximum of $4,050 as funded by Congress. The maximum Pell Grant for the 2005-2006 award year is $4,050.	Complete the Free Application for Federal Student Aid (FAFSA) form. Submit the Student Aid Report and financial aid transcripts from all colleges previously attended.
Supplemental Education Opportunity Grant (SEOG)	Supplements the Pell Grant and uses the same criteria, with need based on a federal formula.	Awards can range up to $4000, but normally in the $500 to $1000 range; varies by school.	Automatic when you submit the FAFSA.
Perkins Loan*	Uses the same criteria as the Pell Grant but requires exceptional financial need.	$20,000 maximum undergraduate borrowing. Federal limit is $4000/year but may be lower in a given school. Repayment begins 9 months after graduation.	Automatic consideration when you submit the FAFSA.

Stafford Loans**: **Subsidized:** awarded on basis of need and no interest until repayment starts. **Unsubsidized:** not awarded on basis of need but interest charged from the time loan is disbursed.	Same criteria as Pell except must be enrolled for 6 credits minimum.	$2625 for freshman, $3500 for sophomore, $5500 for upperclassman.	These loans are direct from the Federal government and/or handled through local commercial lenders such as banks, S&Ls or credit unions.
SMART Grant – pending legislative approval January 2006	Students with full Pell Grants, rigorous HS curriculum and 3.0 min GPA. Must be math, science, engineering, technology or foreign language majors.	Max awards $750 freshman, $1300 sophomore, $4000 junior and senior	School financial aid office has information
Work-Study programs - may be on or off-campus	Based on financial need as determined by the school.	Always the Federal minimum wage but often more; usually paid by the hour.	School financial aid office has information.

This information was accurate as of January 2006 but financial aid is an ever-changing, complex subject. See your school's Financial Aid office for complete details.

* Perkins loans can be completely or partially forgiven if the student enters certain occupations after graduation. These include teaching in designated public schools serving low-income families, teaching special education, teaching in fields designated as teacher shortage areas, becoming an employee of a public or non-profit child- or family-service agency serving high-risk children, becoming a full time nurse or medical technician, serving in the Peace Corp or Vista, or entering certain law enforcement fields. Enlistment in the military also qualifies for loan forgiveness under certain circumstances.

** The criteria to get Stafford Loans are fairly complicated.

For detailed information on Perkins, Stafford and other types of Federal loans, visit:

http://studentaid.ed.gov/students/publications/student_guide/2005-2006/english/index.htm

Can you pay the bill over time?

Schools realize that tuition is a major financial burden for students. That's why many colleges have set up time-payment plans. Details vary by school, of course, but typically the tuition bill is cut into three, four or five equal installment payments spread out over the semester or quarter. Some schools charge a processing or deferral fee to set this up. Some also only do it for the longer Fall and Winter/Spring sessions, and sometimes it is not available for part-time students carrying less than a full credit load. If this sort of arrangement would help you out, check your school's financial aid office for details.

Should you take out a loan?

No one should go into debt unless it's a last resort, but for many people it's either borrow money or not go to school. There are a very wide variety of federal, state and school programs available. The most popular Federal programs are noted above in the chart, but many states and many schools have similar programs as well. If you need to borrow money to attend college, don't stop your information search with the Federal programs.

More and more students are putting tuition and books on their charge cards. Whether this is a good idea or not depends on how you handle credit and debt….and what you think of interest rates that can approach 30%!

Your financial aid package

Once all the appropriate forms are filed - FAFSA for Federal aid and others for state, school and scholarship organizations - your school will have all the information it requires to put together a complete package of financing from all of the sources to which you applied. This may include grants, loans, scholarships, work-study programs, etc. It may also include some contribution from you or your employer. The entire package will be, in the estimation of your financial aid officer, adequate for you to attend their college. If you don't believe that it will be for some reason - changes in your circumstances, errors on their part or some other reason - you need to go back to the financial aid people quickly and review the components of your package one at a time with them. You always have the right to appeal any decision. It is, after all, your college education that is at stake here. Squeaky wheels sometimes do get the grease, and your school may be able to find additional funds somewhere.

Other sources of information

Information on various forms of financial help include your college's financial aid office, high school financial aid offices, libraries, your state representatives, and the local office of your national congressional representatives. Your state and federal representatives probably won't have detailed information in front of them, but they can tell you who to contact to get that information. Your best source of information is probably the college financial aid office.

A good place to start investigating Federal funds is the U.S. Department of Education publication "The Student Guide - Financial Aid." To get a copy, call 1- 800-433-3243 or follow this link, which allows you to email the Department of Education to request a copy: http://studentaid.ed.gov/PORTALSWebApp/students/english/contactus.jsp

Financial aid information on the World Wide Web

There is also a huge amount of financial aid information available on the Internet. Start with these addresses, many of which are linked to other resources.

http://studentaid.ed.gov/students/publications/student_guide/index.html this is the web version of the Federal Student Guide noted above. Contains considerable detail on Federal financial aid programs.

www.fafsa.ed.gov : this is the Free Application for Federal Student Aid (FAFSA) form on the web. You can fill this out and submit it electronically at this site.

http://studentaid.ed.gov/PORTALSWebApp/students/english/index.jsp The Federal Student Aid site noted above.

http://studentaid.ed.gov/students/publications/completing_fafsa/index.html : this site provides help in completing the sometimes-arcane FAFSA form.

http://bcol02.ed.gov/Programs/EROD/org_list.cfm?category_ID=SHE : this site provides a list of state higher education agencies.

Scholarship information on the World Wide Web

There is also no shortage of information regarding possible scholarships. Begin your search at these sites.

The College Board maintains a web site with extensive information on financial aid, scholarships, loans etc. Check it out at http://apps.collegeboard.com/cbsearch_ss/welcome.jsp

You might also want to investigate a web site called Scholarships 101 from Pinnacle Peak Solutions, co-sponsored by Coca-Cola. This site includes information on how to access more than 8,000 funding sources comprised of more than 600,000 individual awards and includes links to dozens of financial aid sites and sources of additional information. http://12.47.197.196/scholarships101/

www.fastweb.com
www.finaid.org
www.salliemae.com
www.collegenet.com

See the References Section for more financial aid web sites.

> "I don't like it that we were poor enough to qualify for financial aid. ....(But) there is enough financial aid, at least for a state college, if you live at home, that you can get an education. And I'm very grateful for that because I couldn't have afforded to put myself through school."
>
> *Karen D. is a single mother of four who originally started school in the early 70s. Some of her 40+ hour/week work schedule was a campus work/study program.*

Federal help by phone

1-800-433-3243: this Federal number provides general information about Federal financial assistance programs, explanations of eligibility requirements, help with the FAFSA form, and a place to order various Federal student aid publications such as The Student Guide. This office is open 8 AM to 8 PM Eastern Time Monday through Friday.

Tax implications

For some people, some or all of the costs of attending college may be fully or partially tax deductible. Tax law is pretty convoluted, and this book is not even going to try to address this issue in any detail. But it might be worth a phone call to your accountant or the Internal Revenue Service to ask if any of your educational expenses might be tax deductible. Self-employed people or owner's of businesses might be able to deduct educational expenses as business expenses. It can't hurt to ask.

Two recent Federal programs - the HOPE Scholarship and the Lifetime Learning Credit - give you income tax breaks. These are dollar-for-dollar reductions in tax liability for higher education expenses. HOPE is a tax credit worth up to $1500 per student for first and second year students enrolled at least half time. The Lifetime Learning Credit is a tax credit of 20% of a family's tuition expenses up to $5000. It is available for virtually any post-secondary education and training. There is much additional information available at:
http://www.ed.gov/offices/OPE/PPI/HOPE/index.html

FAFSA, SAR and other Federal alphabet soup

The Federal FAFSA form is typically the beginning point for all applications for grants and loans. It may take as long as a couple of months for it to go through the system, and the result is something called an SAR, the Student Aid Report. The SAR contains all of the information you provided on the FAFSA, plus information on your eligibility for Federal student aid. It will give you a Pell Grant Index number (PGI) and a Family Contribution (FC) number. If the PGI is above a certain number you are not eligible for a Pell Grant; if it is below that number you are. If you do qualify for a Pell Grant your SAR will have three parts:

Part I is the Information Summary, which gives you instructions on how to review your SAR to make certain it is correct.

Part II is the Information Review Form, which allows you to change any incorrect information on your SAR. Make the changes and return this part. You'll be issued a new SAR in a few weeks.

Part III is the Pell Grant Payment Voucher. This portion is for your school's use. Just give it to them - they'll know what to do with it.

NOTE: The federal government no longer accepts printed FAFSA forms – you MUST file online. Go here to start that process: http://www.fafsaonline.com/

Start your search for bucks early

The FAFSA should be filed as soon after the first of the year as possible. As noted above, you <u>must</u> file on the World Wide Web. Other forms - for state programs, scholarships, etc. - also need to be filed quickly. These sources of money are not bottomless, and it's often first come, first served. And you want to be one of those.

If you are planning on entering school in the fall, you should have all of your paperwork done and in by March if not earlier. Your school's financial aid office can give you the exact dates, but be prepared to spend some time right after Thanksgiving rounding up all the information you need to complete the various forms.

Financial aid workshops

Financial aid is a complicated, time-consuming proposition for most of us. That's why many schools run free workshops periodically. These are usually staffed by the folks from the Financial Aid office, and that's a good place to start looking for the dollars you need.

Even though this subject looks pretty complex, it can be arm-wrestled into submission with some work. There <u>is</u> money around to pay for your college. And you <u>can</u> find it. It just takes time and effort.

Scholarship and financial aid scams

Finding the money to finance your education can sometimes be a long, arduous process. It's easy to become discouraged. And it's even easier to believe that someone else will do it for you....for just a modest amount of your money. While there are some legitimate organizations that provide help in processing the paperwork, there is no shortage of downright scams that promise to get you scholarship money or speed up the loan approval process or get you more money than you appear to be legally entitled to, often in return for an "application fee" or something similar.

Don't do it!

These people have no intention of helping you. They are only interested in helping themselves: to your money. If the financial aid people at your school can't affirm the legitimacy of an organization, don't do business with them. And if they persist in heckling you, you might want to call your local district attorney or state Attorney General.

> **"I plan on probably working 90 hours a week during the summer. That way I can save some money so I won't have to take out as much in loan money next semester."**
> *Jason B., 27, worked a full time job, a part time job and attended school full time.*

CHAPTER 8

Save A Ton of Money - Start At Your Local Community College

> "Even if money were no object, I'd still come here. Because I'm at home here. I love it here. I became comfortable here. I know a lot of the professors, I know a lot of the counseling staff, the support staff, and they're wonderful here. They're here for us."
>
> *Bette B., 40 and the mother of two, started at her local community college in 1997 and earned her AAS degree in 1999. She went on for her Bachelor's and is now working on her Master's.*

The biggest bargain in a college education

The community college (this used to be called junior college) concept was originated early this century by William Harper, president of the University of Chicago. The idea of a college dedicated to the first two years of a four year college education caught on quickly.

Mike Doolin

California has had community colleges since 1907, and now has more than 100 of them. It was such an obviously great idea that it has since been adopted by the rest of the country, and there are now community colleges all over. In my state alone - New York - there are more than five dozen. Nationwide there are nearly 1200 such schools, with about 1600 campuses.

Community colleges offer freshman and sophomore courses - the 100 and 200-level courses that constitute the first two years of a four year, Bachelor's degree college education. According to the American Association of Community Colleges (2006 data) (www.aacc.nche.edu), there are now about 11.6 million students enrolled in community colleges across the country, and 46% of all undergraduates are in community colleges. About 62% of these students attend part-time (less than 12 credit hours/semester). The average student is almost 30 years old. About six in ten are female. About 1/3 of them receive some form of federal or state financial aid. Over 90% of the population of the United States is less than an hour's drive from a community college, and these institutions grant more than 490,000 Associate's Degrees and about 235,000 two-year certificates every year.

Why is the two year community college a good place to start?

To begin with, its courses are typically priced <u>much</u> less than the four year schools in your area. According to the AACC, average annual tuition is less than $200 in about one-third of their member community colleges, between $200 and $1000 in another one-third, and over $1000 in the final third. Nationwide, average yearly tuition is a bit more than $1500. So even the most expensive ones are usually less expensive than typical four year schools. As an aside, I have in front of me catalogs from a number of private four year colleges. On average they are about <u>ten</u> times the cost of a typical community college.

> "(My community college) offered me the remedial classes that I needed to bring me up to par, and I was afraid that the larger colleges wouldn't offer me that. ....I really hate to leave. I've met a lot of really great people here. I have a family here, with the professors, with my advisors, with the other students."
>
> *Joyce M., 36 and a single mother of three, earned her Associate's degree from a local community college with a 3.8 GPA. She later earned a Bachelor's Degree from a private four year school.*

Community colleges, as public institutions, are funded largely by a combination of tuition, state, county and - sometimes - city money. The contribution from tuition can be kept low because the other sources of money are paying most of the bills. Private colleges, on the other hand, receive most of their operating dollars from tuitions. They have no choice but to charge high rates. Private schools do usually have more financial aid available, typically in the form of school grants or scholarships, so it will pay you to investigate both types of schools. In many cases though, you will find that the community college is simply the lower cost alternative for the first two years of your education.

And, as noted earlier, since the first two years of practically any degree program are going to involve many of the same courses no matter where you take them, you might as well take them in a school that's nearby and less expensive.

Stay in the same accreditation conference

Try very hard to find a community college in your area that is in the same accreditation conference as the four year school you will wind up in. The accrediting body for the school is usually listed in the index of the college catalog, and will probably be described in the first few pages. It will be something like Middle States Association of Colleges and Secondary Schools, North Central Association of Colleges and Schools, Southern Association of Colleges and Schools, etc.

Making a preliminary selection of a four year school to transfer into pretty much pushes you into choosing a major or at least a broad course of study early on, but this exercise can be very worth it.

Why is accreditation important? Because you can lose a lot of credits when you transfer from a two year school to a four year college if they are not accredited by the same organization. Unless you move from one part of the country to another, this probably won't be a problem. But be aware that it can be. If it happens, it can be an enormous waste of time and money.

Community colleges have a lot going for them

Community colleges are also good starting choices for many other reasons. With more than 1200 community colleges nationwide, geographic proximity is a major benefit. There are many sections of the country that cannot support a four year school because they do not have the population density necessary. Smaller cities often do not have public four year schools, although they may have private colleges, which tend to be even more expensive.

But nearly all small cities have a community college. If your plans include a Bachelor's Degree, eventually you are going to have to go to a four year school. But if it means a long drive and/or high tuition costs, you will probably want to finish as much work as possible nearby and at lower costs.

2+2 and articulation agreements

Many community colleges have formal arrangements with four year schools in their area that allow all of your credits to transfer directly into the four year institution. If you successfully complete the first two years at the community college, you get to transfer in to the four year school as a first-semester Junior....a clean, neat, uncomplicated transfer.

These programs sometimes have names like "2 + 2", "articulation agreement" or something similar that indicates the alliance between the community college and the four year university. In many cases the two year component requires you to actually graduate from the community college with your Associate's degree - always a good idea anyway - while others create a program for the first two years in the community college that is merely a lower cost mirror image of the first two years you would get if you went directly into the four year school.

In either case, programs like this can keep you from taking a bunch of courses that you don't need or that won't transfer. These sorts of mistakes can cost you a lot of time and money on the front end - by taking courses that don't count - and can cost you more time and money in the Junior and Senior years of your program - by making you repeat courses that you've already taken but did not transfer. If you can get into a "2 + 2" program in your local community college, do it.

These "2+2" programs sometimes have cut off limits for the number of credit hours you can earn at the community college. If you have accumulated more than the limit you are ineligible to apply to the program. Typically the upper limit is between 18 and 32 credits, but it varies by program and school. If this sort of program interests you, check into it in your first semester. Your Adviser will have the details.

If for some reason you miss the credit hour cutoff, you can usually get the same effect by following the 2+2 curriculum inside a Liberal Arts major. Your Adviser will know how to set this up.

> **"I think (this community college) is a great start. The support structure here is great. And it's an excellent school. ... I wish I could do all four years here. If I could, I'd stay here. And financially it's great. You can't beat it."**
>
> *Jason B., 27 and custodial parent of four small children, went to his community college full time, worked a full time job and a part time job.*

Community colleges are full of adult students

Community colleges are also more used to dealing with the so-called non-traditional student...the returning or just-starting adult night-school student, the full-time worker, the single mother trying to get off public assistance, the paroled person trying to get his life back on track. Although the community colleges aren't perfect at handling the widely varied circumstances of this mixed bag of people, they are likely much better at it than most four year schools, which tend to draw a much more traditional (and younger) type of student.

Also, the teachers at community colleges are probably better at teaching, since their primary responsibility is to teach. Their promotions don't depend heavily on doing research or publishing papers and books. The professors in the four year schools worry about these non-teaching tasks a lot, because those things seriously affect their goal of tenure.

You have probably heard the phrase "publish or perish." Many professors in four year schools live by that phrase. The time they spend doing research and writing for publication is time they don't spend preparing for classes or standing in front of the classroom or grading papers or any of the other activities that are directly related to teaching.

Are there more PhDs at the four year schools? Yes, there are. PhDs are comparatively rare on the campuses of community colleges - most teachers have Master's degrees. A 1992 survey (the National Study of Postsecondary Faculty, sponsored by the U.S. Dept. of Education), showed that 61% of those surveyed in community colleges had Master's degrees, about 18% had Bachelor's, and about 16% had Doctorate's. While this is the latest data available for community colleges, the 1999 National Study of Postsecondary Faculty shows that of full time faculty who taught only undergraduate courses in 4-year, non-doctoral-granting institutions, about 93% had at least a Bachelor's Degree, about 84% had at least a Master's, and about 61% had earned a Doctorate. (http://nces.ed.gov/pubs97/97470.pdf)

But the fact is that you are not likely to actually meet many PhDs at a lot of four year schools anyway, particularly for Freshman and Sophomore level classes. The "Docs" and "post-Docs" are usually too busy doing research and writing papers to bother with most of these lower level classes. The ones they do actually teach are usually huge affairs with hundreds of students assembled in cavernous lecture halls. Consequently, a lot of the lower level classes in four year schools are actually taught by grad students and Teaching Assistants.

This isn't universally true. Many four year schools make a real effort to have the lower level classes taught by senior faculty. But the fact that they have to make the effort at all tells you something about the way they are structured.

Most four-year schools offer excellent educations, there is no doubt about that. But if you have a choice of where you are going to take the first two years of classes - and saving many thousands of dollars interests you - you will certainly want to at least check your nearby community college.

For a very complete list of community colleges, visit the American Association of Community Colleges web page at: http://www.aacc.nche.edu/Template.cfm?Section=CommunityColleg eFinder1 .

> **"I'm very satisfied with the education that I've gotten at (my community college) and I know that I'm going to be very prepared to go on to any four year school."**
> *Jason B. earned his Associate's and went on for his Bachelor's.*

CHAPTER 9

How To Save Even More Money

> "I bought a used book the other day. It cost me $36. It was a softcover."
> *Dave P., 49, married and a father, beat cancer and decided to return to college after being away for nearly 30 years.*

This will get expensive if you're not careful

Getting a college education can be a very expensive proposition, make no mistake about that. As noted in Chapter 7, there are some possibilities for getting someone else to pay for some or all of your tuition, through employee reimbursement programs, grants, scholarships, work-study programs and so forth.

But even if you are fortunate enough to qualify for one or more of those opportunities, you will still probably have to lay out a sizable chuck of cash for all the rest of the expenses associated with going to school. Here's a short list:

Tuition	Library cards
Books	Parking Permits
Internet Access	Photo ID fees
School Supplies	Parking Tickets
Application fees	Transportation expenses
Student Association fees	Meals
Lab fees	Expense related to field
Accident or car insurance	trips
Medical service fees	

You can see that there's more to paying for college than just finding a way to cover tuition payments, although tuition is by far the largest single cost. While there is nothing you can do about the various fees that your school is going to charge you, some of those other expenses noted above are somewhat under your control and can be reduced. Let's look quickly at some of them.

Tuition
I'll say it again: In most parts of the country, for the first two years of a four year Bachelor's Degree, your best deal on college tuition is undeniably your nearby community college. Tuition per credit hour at some community colleges is a fraction of what it is at the state or public four year school in the same city, and the dollar difference between community colleges and private schools is staggeringly large.

In nearly every comparison, the tuition at your community college is going to be significantly less than a four year college. And many would argue that the quality of the education is at least equal to – and in some cases, better than – most four year schools.

> "I have had bad luck with used books because people who underline poorly confused me. I thought it was so great - Oh, somebody already underlined! It was worse. So I try to buy books that have as little underlining as possible."
> *Evelyn S., 41 and the mother of two, returned to school after she was disabled on the job. She began at her community college in the mid-1970s, returned a couple of decades later, and eventually transferred to her four year and received her Bachelor's degree.*

Books

College textbooks get more expensive every year. It's not unusual to have to spend many hundreds of dollars a year on books. There are a couple of ways to cut this expense down to manageable size.

The easiest way is to buy used books if you can find them. Many times your campus bookstore will buy used books from students and then resell them. Unfortunately, most bookstores view this as an easy way to make a few extra bucks rather than providing a service for their students, so used books may not be great bargains.

Mike Doolin

And if you do buy used books, go through the ones you pick off the shelf very carefully. Some previous owners will have been better than others in how they treated those books. Some students actually tear out pages. Texts with heavy underlining, marginal notations or a lot of highlighting are not much use. While at first glance it may seem as if the previous owner has done a lot of the work for you in that class, they haven't. Your instructor probably has a different version of what's important in the class. If someone else has already marked up the text extensively, when study time comes around it's going to be difficult to determine what underlines and highlights are yours and which came from the previous owner.

Don't be bashful about posting a notice on school bulletin boards asking to buy used books. You can also, of course, sell your used books to someone else or to the bookstore to raise a few bucks to pay for this semester's requirements.

Revealed! The secret of how to get textbooks without paying for them!

"I haven't paid for any textbooks now for about three years. For 50 cents my downtown library will do a national book search. So I find out what book the professor is going to be using. I can often just call the college bookstore. And I usually try to get the ISBN number.

"(The search) usually takes three or four days, so I do this a week or two before the class starts. The book I'm using now came from Pennsylvania.

"The usual check-out time is three weeks, but the maximum fine for overdue books is only $6.00. So what I do is get the books and simply keep them until the end of the semester to use as textbooks. The maximum fine is $6 per book. And then I turn them in and they OK my library card again. So I've got two textbooks that are costing me a total of $12 for the semester.

"I've gotten books from Los Angeles, Chicago, Louisiana, books from all over. Postage paid. All you have to do is pay your 50 cents for the search fee. It's a service (my library) offers and nobody uses it.

"I've kept this a secret until now, but now that I'm finishing I can tell people."

The student who gave me this tip asked that he/she be kept anonymous, and I am honoring that request. I can't verify if this service is available at all libraries. If your library will do this for you, it could easily save you thousands of dollars over the course of a college education. Of course, there is the ethical consideration of keeping a book longer than expected and depriving someone else of its use.

Another way to reduce book expense is to share books with a friend. This only works well with good friends who are well organized. A third technique is for you and a friend to alternate on some classes: she takes the class one semester, you take it the next. You can split the cost of the required books. I did this for a number of classes with a co-worker who was also in a business major program like I was. We had a lot of classes in common and tried to schedule them alternately. We saved a lot of money over a few years.

But beware: This only works for those classes with stable book requirements. A lot of people who write college textbooks make minor changes in them every couple of years. The cynical among us would say that they do this just to boost sales (and, of course, their income). If you get caught in one of these changes of editions, the version used last semester may not be usable for this semester. Note that not every teacher immediately switches to new editions. You may be able to find a class using the old edition. Don't destroy your schedule hunting for a class using the previous text - it's just not worth it. But it can't hurt to check. A call to the department secretary can probably put you in touch with the instructor teaching a given class. And since books are ordered months in advance – September books are typically ordered in April – your bookstore should be able to tell you what edition of a book is used for a given section of a class.

Some teachers change books every semester. That's fine for the teacher, who doesn't pay for the books. But it's hell on students. It decreases or completely eliminates the market for used books, and you can be sure that just-published books are going to be more expensive than the ones that have been used for a few years. Other things being equal, it might pay to avoid classes using brand-new books. In addition to being more expensive, they sometimes are not available until the class has already started, making it very difficult to stay abreast of what's going on in the class.

Check with your teacher to see which required books are going to be used a lot, and which are going to be used only a little. Then see if the school or a local city library has a copy of the little-used book.

Some teachers also routinely put their textbooks on reserve in the school library. If your teacher is one of these, and you are able to schedule regular visits to the library, you may be able to reduce or eliminate having to buy certain books for certain classes. If your instructor hasn't put the text on reserve, they probably will if you ask them.

While you can almost always get your books in the campus bookstore, that may not be the cheapest place to buy them. If you have Internet access, get the ISBN number for the texts you need and visit www.Amazon.com, www.BarnesandNoble.com or one of the other huge Internet bookstores. In just a few minutes you will know whether their price is competitive with your bookstore's, and how quickly you can get the book. I have personally saved hundreds of dollars on texts by buying them on the Internet, and have been able to find books that my local national bookstores were unable to find.

An alternate to buying new or used at an online bookstore is to check eBay (www.ebay.com) ,where books can be very inexpensive. Make sure that the ISBN number is the same as the one you want.

A few notes of caution regarding books. Books for classes with the same course number and description may not be the same from one semester to the next. And they may not be the same from one teacher to the next, even in the same semester. The "Intro To...." courses are notorious for this, as every professor has his or her own idea of what constitutes a correct book selection for a given course. And most schools give their professors a lot of latitude in selecting books for their courses. If, for example, there were two sections of English 101 side by side on a given night taught by two different instructors, each section might call for totally different books.

If you buy the books you need at the campus bookstore, try to schedule your visit at a time when the day school kids are likely to be somewhere else if possible. The place will be noticeably less crowded and confusing. Buy your books as early as possible. Books are ordered months ahead of time by the professors based on how many sections of a class they are teaching and the average enrollment for a particular section.

If the class doesn't 'make' - educational jargon for not enough students signing up for a particular time period - that particular section will get canceled. That means there will be too many books available. Conversely, some classes may get over-enrolled and the administration will have to put on more sections. And then there won't be enough books. Since book reorders often take several weeks to show up, you'll want to buy your books early.

> "I got a $3000 state grant for adult students. I used it to pay for books and supplies."
> *Kathleen C., 56 and employed full time, started at a community college in the late 1970s. She earned her Bachelor's degree more than two decades later.*

Read the course book descriptions in the bookstore very carefully. Often a shelf will have a label that says something like: "Ms. Smith's English 101, Sections 212 and 213" with an arrow pointing up to a shelf full of books. This looks like a good system, and most of the time it is.

But people make mistakes in labeling, book requirement changes might not get communicated to the bookstore people (who are usually young students in co-op jobs) and sometimes things get moved around. Always recheck your book selection at the cash register before you start shelling out money. Keep your receipt. And then check again with your teacher at the first class session to make certain you have the right texts. Don't unwrap your books or write your name in them until you know for sure you have the correct books. Sometimes a quick phone call to the department secretary to verify the ISBN is all you need.

A word about ISBNs
In some courses there may be more than one standard text. Sometimes texts will be packed with ancillary materials such as CDs, DVDs, maps, dictionaries, style guides, etc. Each of these different versions will have different ISBN numbers, even though the basic texts are identical. Make certain that you know which version has been specified. If the bookstore folks try to give you one with an ISBN number different from the one you believe is correct, ask to speak to the person who buys the texts, or the bookstore manager. They will know for certain which text the professor wants.

Internet Access
If this book had been written just a few years ago, this section wouldn't even be in here. But the Internet has grown so large, so fast, and has become so useful, that it has to be mentioned.

The Net is the world's largest library, with billions of sites and who knows how many pages. Although it is difficult to find some sorts of material on the Internet - some types of up to the minute research as one example - it has nearly everything else. And you'll want to use it.

But to use it you must have a computer system capable of accessing the internet and an account with an Internet Service Provider such as America OnLine, CompuServe, your local telephone company, etc. If you have those things, you're all set. Just fire up your web browser and start looking around.

For those without computer systems and/or Internet access, there are a couple of possibilities. Your school almost certainly has access. The American Association of Community Colleges estimates that more than 95% of its members are connected to the Net. When you register for classes you will probably be given instructions on how to use the college's computer system, including a password for access to the Internet and your personal email account. Most school libraries will have terminals, and in many schools there will be a campus computer center as well.

The second access point will be the public libraries in your city or town. Libraries were quick to jump on the Internet bandwagon, and most public library systems now have terminals, at least in their main facilities if not their branches. You may need a library card to use them, but as a college student you should certainly have one of those anyway. The problem with using library terminals is that you are in competition with your fellow city residents. Some libraries have instituted time limits on the use of their terminals in an effort to give everyone equal access.

A third possibility is an Internet Cafe. These are small retailers who have combined coffee shops or delis with rows of computer terminals hooked to the Internet. You will pay for the privilege of using their equipment, of course, but you may find these locations less crowded than the school or public library.

A final possibility is a commercial copy center. At least one national chain – FedEx/Kinkos (http://fedex.kinkos.com/) offers Internet access at most of their facilities.

And don't overlook the fact that being able to access the Internet from many other locations besides your home allows you to travel on business or pleasure and still be able to do homework, research etc. The rapidly growing use of "hot spots" – wireless access points – allows you to use your wireless-equipped laptop in many locations without the need for a hardwired connection.

> **"I get most of my text books out of the library. I'm kind of known for not buying textbooks. I save a ton of money that way."**
> *Ann H. is 33 and the mother of one child. She took her first two years at her local community college and transferred in to her four year school as a Junior. She earned her Bachelor's degree and is going on for her Master's.*

Parking permits and parking tickets

If you are a college administrator, parking is a wonderful source of extra revenue. You can charge people for the right to park on your campus - a campus they are already paying big bucks to come to through their tuition - and then force them to obey strangely-reasoned, obscure rules that are easy to violate. Then when they do violate those rules, you can charge them scandalous fines for doing so. And if they refuse to pay those outrageous fines, you can just withhold grade cards, transcripts, even forbid them from registering or even graduating.

If you're an administrator, it's a perfect system.

If you are a student, particularly a night school or other part-time student paying most of his or her own way, parking fees and parking tickets are an enormous pain in the tail and a very aggravating, low-life assault on your good humor and already-skinny wallet.

I find the whole concept of campus parking requirements personally offensive, but there is no question that you are going to run into them, so get used to the idea. A few hints are in order.

If you have incredible good luck and can find a way to park off campus and walk to class, do it. The exercise will do you good, and the avoidance of campus parking lots will save you hours of grief, to say nothing of parking tickets. If you can hitch a ride with someone else, or ride the bus, do it. If you have to park on campus, bite the bullet and get the parking sticker. There is no question that it is unfair, unnecessary and immoral to ask you to shell out even more money just to use a parking space, but you have no choice. Well, you do have a choice, but that choice is called parking tickets and you will find them to be very expensive. Get the sticker.

Transportation expenses

It costs money to own and drive a car. As I write this in early 2006, the Federal government allows 44.5 cents per mile for business mileage expenses (although they have a habit of changing this number every year or two.) This is nowhere near what it actually costs to run a car: the true cost is much higher. If you are attending classes several times a week, visiting the campus or city public library a few times a month, doing some work at the campus computer center or writing center, these expenses can add up to large bucks in gas, maintenance, insurance, depreciation, etc. Here are a few ways to keep those expenses under control.

Probably the best way to cut transportation costs is to car pool with one or even several other people. Does anyone else in your company go to your school or one nearby? Your personnel department might be able to put you in touch, or maybe a notice on your company bulletin board will work. Maybe there's someone in your neighborhood going to your school. A few notices on trees and poles might give you a call. And there's probably a ride bulletin board at your school as well.

Public transportation is much cheaper than driving a car. Although it can be a bit inconvenient, taking the bus will definitely save you some money. And if your school is of any size, the bus probably stops right in front of it.

If you have to drive any distance to get to school, you might want to consider getting the most economical car you can find. When I started commuting 75 miles one way, four nights a week to get to classes, it quickly occurred to me that my big Chevy station wagon was probably not an economical choice for transportation. The little 4-cylinder car I bought just to go back and forth to school paid for itself.

Motorcycles and scooters will have the same effect if you can drive them and the weather is cooperative. A bicycle will pretty much eliminate your commuting costs but unless you're in training for the Tour de France, long bike jaunts are probably not a productive way to spend your precious time.

Distance learning courses don't require you to go anywhere: you can sit at home and do them over your computer or TV set, or through your mail box. Chapters 16 and 17 provide more information on these alternatives.

Meals

If you are going to attend classes at night, you are probably going to have trouble getting home in time after work to eat with the rest of the family and still make class on time. If you leave work at 5 PM or so and class starts at 7 PM, you might get your supper at home. If class starts at 5:30 or 6 PM - also very common - you will really have to hustle. Saturday or Sunday classes that run all day present the same problem.

Eating at home is obviously the least expensive way to stay fed, but it isn't the only way. Taking a lunch and <u>dinner</u> from home in the morning works pretty well, since there's usually a cafeteria of some sort in the school. If you are a night school student it probably won't be open by the time you get there, but there will be a table to sit at and a pop or coffee machine. Snacks are another possibility: some fruit or yogurt can tide you over through class until you can get home.

Try to avoid the fast food joints if you can. They're expensive, not always that fast, and that sort of food doesn't do much for your health.

> **"You can spend $300 or $400 for books every semester."**
> *Jason B., 27, went to school full time, had a part time and a full time job, and qualified for Federal and State grants and student loans.*

CHAPTER 10

Budgeting

> "I choose (my local community college) for the cost, the location, and the convenience. After I got there I realized it was a damn good school."
> *Patrick A., 46 and the father of two, cut his work schedule in half and managed to get through school in about 5 years.*

Know what this will cost you before you start

As with any big project, you should start your trip through college with some idea of what it's going to cost you. Monetary surprises are usually not too good for the family budget. Although each school differs in what it charges, there are some general categories of costs which can be anticipated. Let's look at each of these. We talked briefly about all of them in the previous chapter.

Tuition
This will be by far your largest single expense. Your employer may cover some or all of this cost, but you will usually have to pay the tuition up front and get reimbursed for it at the end of the semester, presuming you have a passing grade.

Note that tuition reimbursement programs are becoming less popular with employers as they try to trim costs to remain competitive in the global economy. Whether this is a good idea or not long term remains to be seen. Just don't be surprised if you discover that the tuition reimbursement program you thought your company had is now a thing of the past.

As noted elsewhere in this guide, community colleges usually offer the best value in tuition costs, and have per credit hour costs that are often <u>much</u> less than the cost of a four year school. Since you will probably be attending less than full time, you will normally be charged by the credit hour or course, rather than by the semester or quarter. Tuition charges will always be listed in the college's catalog.

Books

Also usually a large expense. As detailed in the previous chapter, there are ways to reduce the cost of books somewhat. Buying new books for a class is always the most expensive way to go, and may typically cost you $100 or more per class. The only way to get an exact cost is to visit the bookstore and check the actual price of each required book.

But don't stop there, and don't buy them there, at least not right away. Write down the title, the edition, the author and the ISBN number. The ISBN (International Standard Book Number) will usually appear on the bar code on the rear cover of the book, and always appears on the same page as the copyright information, normally the first page of the book. Take this information and give your local chain bookstore a call for price and delivery information. Try your library. And check www.Amazon.com or www.BarnesandNoble.com on the world wide web. Going to eBay (www.ebay.com) or other auction sites is usually worth the effort. A little shopping around a few weeks before school starts may save you a lot of money, particularly if you can find the books you need at a library.

Fees

These vary all over the map. Some schools charge for things other schools give you for free. You can usually expect to pay a non-refundable application or registration fee, a parking fee, a student services or student association fee, possibly a student ID card and/or library card fee, perhaps an accident insurance charge and various lab fees for courses that require them. Some schools impose a flat charge for each fee, while others charge by the credit hour. In total you are probably going to have to part with $100 or more per semester for fees and additional charges over and above tuition costs.

> "I knew that I couldn't earn enough to pay our bills. So I had to take out the subsidized loans."
> *Karen D., 46 and a divorced mother of four, originally started college in the early 70s. She earned her Bachelor's Degree while working 40+ hours a week.*

Mileage

Unless you live within walking distance of your school, are willing to take public transportation, or are enrolled in distance learning courses, you are probably going to have to drive to class several times a week, plus trips to the library, the computer center and so forth.

The federal government currently allows businesses to write off mileage at the rate of 44.5 cents per mile, but realistically this is less than half of what it actually costs to run a car if you include depreciation and the cost of insurance and maintenance. Your out-of-pocket expense for gas and routine maintenance is probably going to be on the order of 20¢+ per mile. But remember that your real expense, over time, will be much higher. Eventually those extra miles on the car are going to create additional wear and tear that you will have to pay for in increased maintenance.

Meals

If you are primarily taking night school classes, you might get lucky and have a schedule that allows you to eat at home between the time you leave work and the time you get to class. If you can squeeze in a day school class here and there, that's even better. But regardless of what your schedule is - and it will probably change every semester - be prepared to have to cover some meals away from home. The cost should be built into your school budget.

Let's go through a typical semester budget:

Fall Semester Budget:	
Tuition: 6 credits x $125/credit =	$750.00
Books:	150.00
Registration Fee:	25.00
Student Fee:	40.00
Health Fee:	15.00
Parking Fee:	40.00
Auto Expense @ 20¢/mi: 20 miles round trip x 2 trips/wk x 16 wks:	96.00
or Public Transportation:	------
Misc auto (library, research etc)	32.00
or Public Transportation:	------
Meals ($8/wk x 16 wks):	128.00
	$1276.00

If you are fortunate enough to be reimbursed for tuition, you will get that $750 back, leaving you with a net expense of just $526. This works out to be only $32.88 per week for a 16 week semester. While that's not a lot of money for a college education, you still have to find it in your pocket and figure out a way to subtract it from the overall family budget without serious damage to the rest of your fiscal responsibilities.

Remember that you may be able to pay tuition in three, four or even five installments. You need to investigate this option early on, and set it up in advance if it's offered. If it is, you should probably take it. There may be a partial payment fee attached to this, but it is usually a better deal than putting the whole tuition bill on your credit card, which is also often a possibility. Your school's Admission, Records and Registration or Financial Aid office will tell you if such a plan is available to you.

For budgeting purposes, also note that while some of the costs can be spread over the entire semester - meals, driving costs, maybe tuition - some of the expense is going to have to be paid up front, before school actually starts. Your school may not allow you to pay student and parking sticker fees and the like over time. And book and supplies expenses are going to come out of your pocket in their entirety before you ever set foot in the classroom. Some cash flow management is in order here.

Here's a form you can use for your own budgeting:

_____ Semester, 200___ Budget:

```
Tuition:     __ credits x $__/credit =        $ _____
Books:                                          _____
Registration Fee:                               _____
Student Fee:                                    _____
Health Fee:                                     _____
Parking Fee:                                    _____
Other Fees _____:                    _____
Auto Expense @ __¢/mi: __ miles
  round trip x __ trips/wk x __ wks:            _____
or Public Transportation:                       _____
Misc auto (library, research etc)               _____
or Public Transportation:                       _____
Meals ($_/wk x __ wks):                         _____

    Total:                                      _____

Less Tuition Reimbursement:
    _____

    Net Cost:
    _____
```

Going to college is never cheap. Even if you are fortunate enough to qualify for grants, scholarships, employer reimbursement programs and low interest deferred loans, you still have to come up with sizable amounts of money every semester just to cover books, supplies, transportation and meal expenses. Family budgets that are already tight can feel the strain. Budgeting in advance - and then having the discipline to stay on that budget - can minimize surprises and keep stress to a minimum.

> **"Time, energy and money are the issues confronting adult students. And probably time and energy are the larger of the three. Not to suggest that money is not an issue. But I see people with plenty of money who can't figure out how to make it work because of the time and energy issues."**
> *Sharon Grigsby recruits adult students for Empire State College, one of the very first non-traditional, non-residential colleges in the country and probably the most successful.*

CHAPTER 11

Time Management

> "I think the biggest problem was time. Just having a family, working, and then going to school. Time has probably been my biggest problem."
> Jason B., 27, had four small children, a full time job, a part time job, and went to school full time.

Time
None of us has enough of it

We're only allotted so much of it, then life itself is over. Unfortunately, we never know exactly how much time we have on Earth. So we're never sure about what activities should be given priority. Will we still have time to do Activity A tomorrow if we do Activity B today? We just don't know.

What is certain is that if you decide to go to college as an adult you are going to have to learn to manage your time much more efficiently than the average person. You are going to have to juggle an activity - school - that will absorb large amounts of time, while still fitting in all of the other things that are currently in your schedule: work, your family, social life, etc.

And since going to school is an activity that those around you are probably not experiencing themselves, you are going to have to learn to get the maximum benefit out of the time you do spend on school work while still justifying that time to your family and friends. And still find time to pay attention to them and their needs.

This is not an easy assignment. But how well you succeed at this juggling act is going to have a great effect on how well you do in school.

If you are not already a fairly well organized person, you are going to have to learn to be. Or you will probably fail at going to college. That is the simple fact. You have to find ways to make time for attending classes, studying, trips to the library, researching and writing papers, etc. If other activities continually get in the way of those, the critical school projects won't get done. Soon you'll be earning Ds and Fs instead of As and Bs. And shortly after that you'll be out of school, hundreds or thousands of dollars poorer. And no closer to the degree.

The choice is yours. If earning a degree is important enough to you, you will find the time to make it happen. This book and others like it can help, by showing you ways to analyze your activities, rearrange your schedule and select the tasks that are most important. But only you can actually <u>do</u> those things that move you toward your degree goal.

Let's get started...

Start by learning what you're spending time on now

Begin finding the time to go to school by finding out what you are spending your time on now. The Daily Time Analysis Form in this chapter can help.

Start keeping track of your activities, a day at a time. Recording time spent in ten minute increments will give you a good snapshot of what you are doing currently. Because most people's schedules vary somewhat week to week, you may find it helpful to track more than one week's worth of activities.

The trick to doing this exercise is to be very honest with yourself. Record every activity, no matter how trivial or how important. Time management is really just a matter of discipline, and this is a good opportunity to refine your discipline skills. Be honest with yourself: write down everything you do.

At the end of a week or two or three, you'll have a detailed record of where all of your time has gone. This is valuable information, because now we're going hunting, and our quarry is minutes that add up to hours. We're looking for time wasters or time spent doing activities that could now be used for school.

> **"Learning time management was something I had to do because I've never been a very structured person. So I did have to learn how to structure my life."**
> *Lorene K, 41, worked a full time job and went to school full time.*

Daily Time Analysis Form

	Sun	Mon	Tues	Wed	Thu	Fri	Sat	Total
Your Job Time at work Driving Work at home Other activities *Total Hours*								
Your Leisure Activities TV/Movies Reading Socializing Hobbies Outdoor Volunteering Phone/cell calls Internet/www Computer Games Seminars, classes Cultural events Other activities								
Total hours								

The Success Manual For Adult College Students

	Sun	Mon	Tues	Wed	Thu	Fri	Sat	Total
Your Daily Life Sleeping								
Eating								
Personal grooming								
Housework & laundry								
Attending kids' activities								
Cooking								
Shopping								
House/lawn maintenance								
Managing money, paying bills, etc.								
Auto maintenance								
Misc. chores								
Running errands								
Other daily activities								
Total hours								

> "The biggest thing that's suffered is the house, as far as cleanliness. We've had to learn to let go of it. We don't live in squalor, but we don't harp that much on things laying around any more. And you get a chance to see how much time and effort you put into trying to make the house real clean. It's just going to get dirty again with the kids running around."
>
> *Rich B., 44, is the father of six kids. He went to school at a non-residential, non-traditional college.*

Finding the time wasters

All of us waste time. We spend too much of it watching TV, playing computer games or cruising the internet, polishing the car, tending the garden, or just goofing off. Spend too much time in these non-essential activities and there is no time left for the more important things, like working on a college education.

But maybe we should all waste just a little time, if for no other reason than our lives are so full of minute-to-minute responsibilities. When we're doing something mindless - watching game show re-runs, playing another game of Solitaire on the computer - we're taking a much-deserved break from all of those adult responsibilities. And that little break gives us a rest.

It's when the little breaks become long ones that we really begin to waste time, and what started out as restful relief from our adult world turns into a world unto itself, where we have no responsibility.

Those are the activities you should look for on your completed Daily Time Analysis Form. While there are ways to make more efficient use of the time we use for necessary activities - shopping, cooking, cleaning, etc - we can get the biggest time reward simply by eliminating a lot of time wasting activities.

Look at your form. Is there a lot of TV watching on it, say more than a couple of hours a week? Kill your TV set! Are you spending hours reading trashy romance novels? Trash 'em! Is your car always so clean that it's ready for display in a museum? Hide the polish! Is your lawn so manicured that professional golfers beg to practice on it? Plant some weeds!

You get the point. All of us have activities that we spend too much time on, things that really aren't all that important. Scrutinize your Daily Time Analysis Form for areas of your life that have a lesser priority than college. Collectively these areas probably add up to many hours a week. How much time you actually need to go to college will depend mostly on your class load, but right this minute we're just searching for chunks of wasted time that we can allocate to school. How much did you find?

Squeezing time out of essential activities

Although all of us waste some time, most of our busy adult lives are full of activities that simply have to be done. Someone expects us to do them. Life itself expects them. For most of us, work is pretty much a given: there's not a lot of slack there. It would be difficult for most of us to save any significant amount of time from work every day.

So if we are to save any more time, we need to look in other areas, at other activities that are still required, but may have the potential of being handled in shorter periods of time.

The Daily Time Analysis Form has a number of them, including sleeping/napping, eating, personal grooming, housework and laundry, attending kids' activities, cooking, shopping, house/lawn maintenance, managing money, paying bills, auto maintenance, miscellaneous chores, running errands, etc.

> "My family realizes that school is my top priority as far as my life is concerned right now. They juggle their things that need to be done around my schedule for school."
>
> Linda W., 41 and the mother of one child, started college in 1979 at her local community college. She earned her Associate's degree in the late 1990s and a Bachelor's degree several years later. She eventually expects to earn a Master's.

Some of these are probably not up for modification. As one example, you probably shouldn't try to cut back on attending your kids' school and recreational activities - your college load is going to cut into the amount of time you can spend with your kids anyway, and you probably don't want to reduce that any more.

But there are certainly some things that can be done more efficiently, or done less often. Maybe you don't need to cut the grass once a week. Maybe three times a month is adequate. And that half hour or hour you save can be redirected toward school work. Combining errands can often be a big time (and money) saver. A few minutes spent planning routes and activities can usually pay big time dividends.

Maybe some things don't even have to be done by you any longer. Perhaps your partner or one of the older kids can learn to do laundry or make simple meals....and they should know how to do those things anyway. Maybe someone else should be in charge of running the vacuum cleaner or changing bed linen or raking leaves or picking up the dry cleaning on Thursday. Every household is different, of course, but the point is that if you spend all of your available time in the service of other family members, you will never find the time for yourself and school.

> **"When I really, really have to have the time, my family is very supportive."**
> *Patrick A., 46 and the father of two small children, worked about 20+ hours a week and managed to go to school full time.*

Learn to do two (or more) things at once

Many years ago, right after I was discharged from the U.S. Navy, I got a job working as a barboy in a very busy bar at a famous Southern California tourist attraction. The day I started, the lead bartender who was my boss chastised me for walking from one end of the bar to the other. Why? Because I didn't have anything in my hands. I had made the 30 foot trip and not taken anything with me. I had only done one thing - walked the length of the bar - when I could have done two - walked the length of the bar and carried something at the same time.

It was a lesson I never forgot.

It is possible to do two things at once. And although one of those things will usually be something small and relatively unimportant, it is something that would still absorb time, whether it is done by itself or in concert with something else. And because it is small, it can be done with no real expenditure of mental energy.

Perhaps some examples are in order. The phone rings. It's your sister, brother, best friend, mother, husband, wife, partner, etc. You know you're going to be on the phone for at least a few minutes. If you have a portable or cell phone - wonderful devices, by the way - you can wander around and get a few other things done while you're chatting: load/unload the dishwasher, sort through the mail, wipe off the kitchen countertops, transfer a load of laundry, put some things into the recycling box, etc., etc.

If you're on your way from one part of the house to another, grab something that needs to be moved and take it with you. It hasn't cost you much more energy than walking empty-handed, and you've saved the time needed to go back later and move that thing, whatever it was.

These habits take some getting used to, but soon you'll find that you unconsciously are doing two things at once. And the time-savings can be significant.

**Fit the small jobs
into small time spaces**

Our lives as adults are filled with chores and tasks and things that need to be done. Some are very important: our jobs, as one example. Others are not so important, and can be moved around in our schedules quite a bit. A trip to the grocery store might fit into this category. And some chores are just very small. They can be shoehorned in almost anywhere: wiping down the countertop, folding the laundry, picking up the living room.

> "I'm always doing something else while I'm studying and I don't need quiet. ...I'm cooking and doing laundry. I listen for the wash to stop so I can transfer it to the dryer or put it on the hanging racks. I'll read three chapters and then go clean the bathroom. ...When I have a few minutes to do something, then it gets done."
> *Karen D., a 46 year old mother of four, started college in 1972. She eventually earned her Bachelor's degree nearly three decades later.*

These small jobs can be done very quickly, sometimes in just seconds or a minute or two. These tasks still take time, and collectively they may add up to several hours a week. But you probably don't need to schedule them - you can just do them whenever you have a moment or two. People who successfully manage busy, crowded schedules use this tactic a lot, filling the idle moments that we all have between larger chores by doing the smaller ones. It's a good trick. And it works.

Deanne Organizes Her Life

I have lists like you wouldn't believe, all over the house. Everybody laughs at me, but it's the only way I can do it. I even have to write down dusting, vacuuming, mopping, otherwise it won't get done. It just won't get done.

I write down the exact homework I have to do. I'll make a list for a week, then I'll have a separate list for particular days. I have a calendar that I carry with me, and I also have one for the whole family in the house. That's basically how I keep it all organized.

So at any given moment I know pretty much where I have to be and what I have to do. Because I write it all down. And if it doesn't get written down, forget it. It's done. It's lost.

Deanne L., 39, married and the mother of two, started school in the late 1970s at her local community college. She transferred to a four year state college nearly twenty years later and earned her Bachelor's degree. She now has a Master's degree.

**Buy a scheduler
or personal calendar**

Successful time managers, whether students or busy executives, almost all use some written form of scheduling. Any office supplies store will have several different types on their shelves. Some of them are desk-sized, while others hang on a wall or fit in your pocket. Choose one that seems right for your circumstances. Most of the students interviewed for this book – and many that I see either in classes or in my school's Advising Center - use pocket sized versions combined with a wall calendar-type that they keep at home. The DayTimers company (www.daytimers.com) is one of the most popular suppliers of schedulers and calendars, but there are others. Your computer probably has some calendar/alarm/scheduling capabilities as well, but you might have to look for them.

Some students I've known used as many as three calendars, keeping one at work as well as one at home and one in their pocket or purse. This might present coordination problems, making sure that all versions had the same information, but it didn't seem to bother the students interviewed.

The Weekly Planning Grid in this chapter is a typical personal planning tool. Most commercial versions look something like this. Some give you just a day at a time, while others present a week or an entire month. The concept is the same no matter how much time is visible at once.

The way these are used is pretty self-evident. Activities are just filled into the spaces on the grid: Bio class 7 - 10 PM Wed.; Susie's ballet lesson 3:30 - 4 PM Thurs. Accounting test Mon 4/14. Many of us already use a wall calendar to schedule things like major social or family events, birthdays, anniversaries, etc., so the idea of blocking out the time periods reserved for school and its activities doesn't really take much re-training for most students.

The key to success here is to make sure you write everything down on the planner. <u>Everything</u>! Class meeting times are obvious, but there are a lot more activities associated with going to school that will also absorb time.

And if you are a typically frantic adult trying to sandwich college into an already busy life, you need to be religious about writing down <u>all</u> of your school activities: library and research sessions, study times, tests, reading assignments, due dates for papers and projects, team meetings and so forth.

Note that many of these activities can be picked up off the class syllabus you get at the very beginning of the semester. The syllabus will give you important dates during the semester: test dates, time spans to cover certain chapters in your text, field trips, etc. As soon as you get the syllabus, transfer all of the critical dates into your planning calendar. In pencil. Even teachers can sometimes change their minds.

"I have an appointment book that I live by. I used to be really kind of helter skelter with sticky notes all over the place. But now I've got this appointment book and I just live by it. I write all my classes down. ...I write everything down whether it's school, work or personal life. And I keep it with me. I have a briefcase and it goes with me to lunch, it goes with me to home, and it's on my desk while I'm at work. It's always there."

Kevin R., 34 with two children, worked a full time job and took two classes a semester. He started at a community college in the late 1980s, transferred in to a four year state university in the mid-1990s as a Junior, and got his Bachelor's degree in the late 1990s. He went on for a Master's.

Typical Weekly Planning Grid

Day Time	Mon	Tues	Wed	Thurs	Fri	Sat	Sun
6:00 AM							
6:30							
7:00							
7:30							
8:00							
8:30							
9:00							
9:30							
10:00							
10:30							
11:00							
11:30							
12:00 N							
12:30 PM							
1:00							
1:30							
2:00							
2:30							
3:00							
3:30							
4:00							
4:30							
5:00							
5:30							
6:00							
6:30							
7:00							
7:30							
8:00							
8:30							
9:00							
9:30							
10:00							
10:30							
11:00							

Time management will be the most critical skill you learn as an adult student. If you learn it well - if you can develop the strategies required to fit college into your already-very-busy schedule - you will probably do very well. The students interviewed for this book, the hundreds of students described by the adult counselors I talked with, and the many thousands more I've seen in classes and my Advising Center, all had one thing in common: they were all good time managers. Every single one of them.

And oh yeah. They all had one other thing in common: they were all successful college students. Is there a connection? What do you think?

> **"What problems do most adult students face when they decide to return to school and how do they solve them? Juggling is the short answer. All of the responsibilities: work and family and church and civic organizations, or whatever, and school on top of that. It's a common thread for any adult student anywhere. How to make it happen. Where do you get the time to study?"**
> *Sharon Grigsby recruits adult students for Empire State College, the State University of NY's non-traditional, non-residential college.*

CHAPTER 12

Make Sure You Know What You Have To Take Before You Actually Take It

> "I graduate in May. I should have graduated over the summer. But the first semester I was here I took 16 credits that I shouldn't have taken. And those don't count towards my degree. So I had to go back and retake these other classes. ...I was really upset when I found out that I had to come back here again this semester."
>
> *Jason B. gives us a cautionary tale about what might happen when you pick courses without the help of an experienced adult student adviser or an approved class schedule.*

You can waste a lot of time & $$ taking the wrong courses!

As suggested later in Chapter 15, you should probably start your college career slowly by taking a single course, preferably one you have some interest and/or experience in. If you can manage to make this starter class one of the required, basic ones like English, Math, Psychology, Sociology, etc., that's even better.

Taking a single class is easy. You just register, give them your money, buy the book and you're in school. The process will be pretty simple, and hopefully the class will be fun, motivating you to go back for more.

But from that point on you need to be much more careful about what you take and when you take it. It's very easy to get sidetracked in this process, taking classes that you either don't need for your degree or ones that won't transfer if you are starting in a two-year community college and plan to finally transfer into and graduate from a nearby four-year university.

Look through your college catalog. There are literally hundreds of courses being offered at any given time. The most recent catalog for the community college I teach and advise in lists nearly 1300 courses!

This huge course offering is pretty typical, and this large amount of choice is both a blessing and a curse. A blessing because of the very wide selection of topics you can choose from. A curse for the same reason: You only need a comparatively few of this giant selection – only about 40 altogether from your Freshman year to graduation with a Bachelor's degree.

Some of these courses are absolutely required of everyone, from the Business majors to the Art majors to the Pre-Meds and Pre-Laws and everyone in-between. These are the core courses, and if your college catalog is at all well organized, it will be easy for you to tell which courses these are. They will probably include English Literature and Writing, Math, Social Science, Natural Science, Humanities, Fine Arts, and Phys Ed. In more and more schools you may also be required to take courses in contemporary issues, basic computer skills, Women's Studies and/or a course about minorities or Third World countries. A foreign language is also becoming a requirement in many schools (and Spanish and Chinese are good choices these days.) In some curriculums these courses will fall into the electives category, while in others they will be classed as General Studies courses. But in either case you will probably have to take many if not all of them.

Other courses belong to your major, and will be listed in the catalog under the heading for that specialization. If you are majoring in Business, for example, your required Business Department courses will probably include a variety of Accounting, Finance, Marketing, Business Law, Economics, Statistics and Management courses.

Between the core courses that everyone is obligated to take and the department courses that make up your major, you will probably end up taking about 20 courses - about 60 hours.

The other 60 hours/20 courses you need for a BA/BS degree will usually be electives. But many programs require certain electives to come from certain disciplines, so there is some loss of flexibility. You can't just take 60 hours worth of randomly chosen electives and expect them to qualify, because they won't.

Are you getting confused?

Of course you are. Welcome to the club. That's the whole point of this chapter. With hundreds, perhaps thousands, of courses to choose from in most schools, it is relatively easy to accidentally take a class that doesn't count toward your degree, either because it is just not allowed for credit in your particular major area or because it is considered equivalent to something you have already taken.

During your trip through college you will see dozens of classes that look like they might be fun and interesting to take. And they probably would be. You always wanted to learn Chinese Cooking? There's probably a class in it. Want to know more about how your car runs or how to fix your computer when it crashes? Want to brush up on your Spanish for that vacation trip to Costa Rica? Your school probably has those classes too.

But don't take them!

Not unless you know with absolute certainty that they will count toward your degree. Or understand that because they don't count, they will lengthen your time in school.

If you are a typical part-time adult student, even a two class mistake could cost you an entire semester, to say nothing about the money you spent on tuition and books and parking and the energy that went into studying and passing those classes.

> "Here, everybody gets a letter every semester. This is what you've taken, this is what you still need to take."
> Kathleen C. describing the system her college uses to keep students on track.

So how do you know which courses to take?

Talk to an adviser or counselor. As soon as you finish your first course - perhaps even before you take any course - get an appointment with an adviser. If there is a special program aimed at "adult", "non-traditional", or "returning" students, see if that program has special advisers. If it does, you'll want to talk with one of them, because they will have the necessary background to understand your special circumstances and needs as an adult student. And check the college's web site. Sometimes there will be a separate section devoted to adult students, listing resources, people, departments, contact phone numbers etc.

When you have that meeting, make certain that your counselor understands exactly what it is you are trying to accomplish. Before you go to that meeting, write down your personal college goal. It will probably look something like this:

My College Goal:

I want to get an AS (Associate's) Degree in Business (or Nursing or Art or Engineering etc.) from Neighborly Community College and then transfer into Nearby Friendly University as a Junior to pursue a Bachelor's Degree in Business (or Meteorology or French, etc.). I expect this process to take six years (or five or whatever) and I will never be able to take day school classes because I work during the day (if that's true). I want my program structured around night school, weekend or distance learning classes and further want help determining if I can apply any previous life experience or learning to get credit for any required courses, or if I could test out of any classes.

With written guidance like this from you, spelling out your specific goals and time frame and choice of schools and majors, your adviser should have no trouble putting together a program that will lead you, efficiently, one class at a time, directly to the degree you want. This planning process won't happen in just a few minutes, and it might take more than one meeting. It might even have to be spread over a semester or more, with the first goal being the Associate's degree (if you start at a community college), followed by the program for the next two years.

> "The school gave me a printout of what I needed when I got there. They said, these are what you need. Then I plotted out how I might take them. The adviser reviewed it and said, you can test out of this and test out of this. And he went down the row and suggested, these courses are really heavy in work, why don't you split them up and match them this way."
>
> *Valerie G., 38 and the mother of two, worked a full time job and took two courses per semester for a long time. She started school in the late 1970s and transferred into a four year university about two decades later. She graduated with a Bachelor's degree in the late 1990s.*

Be very careful during this planning process to watch for classes that have prerequisites, as many courses do. (The prereqs will be listed in the course descriptions in your college catalog.) Missing a prereq because of poor scheduling can cause you to blow your overall time schedule. It won't take more than one or two instances like this before you add an entire <u>year</u> to your schedule.

During your adviser's meeting go over the prerequisites one at a time. Make absolutely certain that these required classes are available when you need them. Note that some classes may only be offered <u>once</u> a year. If you need a class like this, pay <u>very</u> close attention to scheduling. Ask to see previous course schedules. Find out how many times per year the school actually plans on offering that class.

Other classes may only be offered at times when you will simply not be available to take them. This is a common problem for night school students who run into classes only offered during the day. The time to spot and correct situations like these is before they become problems. A careful, detailed, class-by-class analysis of every class you need and every prereq required is the only way to circumvent these difficulties.

Review the classes offered at auxiliary campuses. Many schools have satellite branches in other parts of your city or county. Consider classes in other formats: the Internet, correspondence, TV, etc. Information on these possibilities is in Chapters 16, 17 and 18.

Once you have decided what major you want to pursue and have gotten a schedule from your adviser, have him or her put it **in writing**, detailing every class for every semester, as far out into the future as possible. It should be signed by them and dated. Make sure you personally keep a copy of this proposed schedule and that another copy is put into your academic records.

> **Kevin has a different take on degree planning**
>
> "My course plan is written down, but I had to create it myself. My adviser was not much help. I switched advisers a couple times and never found any of them to be of great help to me. It seems like they have too many students that they have to advise.
>
> Each one seems to have a generic plan for what they think each student should be doing. And they don't really want to tailor it to the individual student.
>
> They kind of say, make sure you get this, this, and this, and this course, and blah blah blah. They haven't been much help. For my whole college career I've had to guide myself. And I've heard that complaint from a lot of other students."

Kevin R. was a night school student for his entire college career, usually taking two courses a semester. He transferred into a four year university as a Junior and graduated with his Bachelor's.

This class schedule becomes your Bible

DO NOT deviate from it! Take the classes in the order indicated. If you find an elective that isn't on your list but looks interesting, or may have the potential to speed your trip toward your degree, go back to your adviser to make sure that this new course will substitute exactly in content and hours for the one on your approved schedule. And that it doesn't mess up the prerequisites you have already taken or may need. And then get that change in writing.

A big grid on the wall of your study room is a great tool to mark your progress and quickly show what holes are left to fill. A schedule for a year (for a Business student in this case) might look something like this:

Semester	Fall 2006	Inter-session	Spring 2007	Summer I 2007	Summer II 2007
Courses/ credits	Eng 101: 3 Mth 104: 3	Bio 115: 3	Eco 111: 3 Acc 101: 3	Eco 112: 3 Acc 102: 3	Acc 210: 3
Total credits	6	9	15	21	24

Course Key:

Eng 101: English 101 - no prerequisite

Mth 104: Intermediate Algebra - requires HS algebra and trig – OK

Bio 115: Intro to Biology - no prerequisite

Eco 111: Intro to Microeconomics - requires Mth 104 - OK Fall 06

Acc 101: Principles of Accounting I - requires HS algebra - OK

Eco 112: Intro to Macroeconomics - requires Eco 111 – OK Spring 07

Acc 102: Principles of Accounting II - requires Acc 101 – OK Spring 07

Acc 210: Intermediate Accounting - requires Mth 104 and Acc 102. - OK Fall 06 and Summer 07.

I used a grid like this for very semester I was in school. In my case, that was a lot of semesters. Every time I completed a course, I took a black magic marker and just filled in the cell on the grid. The white spaces were the courses I still had to take. At a glance I could tell exactly how far along I was toward my goal, how many hours I had already earned, what courses I still needed to take, when they were being offered, what the prerequisites for those courses were, and when I had taken those prerequisites.

The point of this entire discussion is to encourage you to PLAN AHEAD. Time is probably a critical issue for you, just as it is for most adult students. And while you will quite likely really enjoy going to college, you probably don't have the time to be taking courses that are merely fun but don't do anything to move you along toward your degree goal. A few hours spent studying your college catalog and meeting with an experienced adult student adviser can save you from making some very time consuming mistakes.

> "I pretty much followed the format from (my community college) right through (my current college). It's preset for me. I go over it with my adviser every semester. In fact, that's a requirement. We have to talk to our adviser every semester before we sign up for classes. To just sort of insure that you're not taking classes you don't need. None of us can afford that."
>
> *Linda W., 41, started at her community college in the very late 1970s, earned her Associate's degree about 20 years later, transferred to her four year school as a Junior, and earned her Bachelor's degree in the very late 1990s.*

Some typical majors and the courses they require

Here are a couple of typical majors, both taken from the catalog for my community college. The first is for Liberal Arts; the second is for Business. These are for Associate's degrees.

Mike Doolin

A.S Degree in Liberal Arts:
62 credit hours minimum

Humanities, 9 credit hours
English 101 (College Composition)	3	
Literature Elective	3	
Humanities Elective	3	9

Social Sciences, 12 credit hours
Any four social science courses	12	12

Natural Science & Math, 11 credit hours
One Math course (Math 150 or higher)	3 - 4	
Two Natural Science courses	6 - 8	11

Electives, 28 – 29 credit hours
Any unrestricted catalog course*	28 – 29

Health Ed/Physical Ed, 2 credit hours
Any Health or Phys Ed class	2	2

62 Credit Hours Minimum

*Courses in Automotive Technology, Nursing, Massage Therapy, Dental Hygiene and Radiology are restricted to students in that major.

A.S. Degree in Business Administration:
64 credit hours minimum

Humanities, 9 credit hours
English 101 (College Composition)	3	
Literature Elective	3	
Humanities Elective	3	9

Social Science, 12 credit hours
Eco 111 Principles of Microeconomics	3	
Eco 112 Principles of Macroeconomics	3	
Social Science Electives	6	12

Natural Science & Math, 12 credit hours
Mth 165 College Algebra or higher	3	
Natural Science Elective	3	
Math (Mth 160 or higher) or Natural Science Electives	6	12

Business, 23 credit hours
Acc 101 Principles of Accounting I	4	
Acc 102 Principles of Accounting II	4	
Bus 104 Introduction to Business	3	
Bus 201 Business Law	3	
Bus 204 Business Management	3	
Mar 101 Principles of Marketing	3	
Business Elective	3	23

Electives, 6 credit hours
Any unrestricted catalog course*	6

Health Ed/Physical Ed, 2 credit hours
Any Health or Phys Ed class	2

64 Credit Hours Minimum

*Courses in Automotive Technology, Nursing, Massage Therapy, Dental Hygiene and Radiology are restricted to students in that major.

These two short examples illustrate the sort of listings you will find in your college catalog. Note that while there are significant differences between these two majors, there are also considerable similarities. Both require 9 hours of Humanities and 2 hours of Health and Phys Ed. Both require 12 hours of Social Science, but the Liberal Arts degree gives you 4 electives while the Business major specifies two of these courses. Both require about the same amount of work in Math and Science, but Liberal Arts gives you more choice as to what these courses will be. And Business only gives you 6 hours of Electives – no surprise since Business requires 23 hours of core Business courses.

See an Adviser
Now

The examples above are only for the first two years of a four year Bachelor's degree. You can see that sorting all this out could get fairly complex. You might be able to unravel all of these requirements without help, but the odds are pretty good that even with your college catalog in front of you, you have no clue what an appropriate Humanities Elective might be, what courses are Business Electives, or what might – or might not – be a Natural Science course.

Your Adviser, of course, knows the answers to all of these questions and many more. He or she has taken lots of seminars at their school that deal with the intricacies of course selection, majors, transfers, prerequisites and all the rest of the areas that could cause you to take classes that won't work for you. You've paid their salary – it's in your tuition. Schedule an appointment with an Adviser now. It'll be the best hour you ever spent in college. And it will save you countless more.

CHAPTER 13

How Adults Learn

> "I tend to get away from those (classes) that do strict lecture. I have to have some hands-on. I learn by hands-on."
> *Joyce M, 36, earned her Associate's degree and eventually went on for a Master's. She was head of her community college Honor Society and had a 3.8 GPA.*

We're different from the kids

As a race we've been learning for hundreds of thousands of years, and our formal educational systems in both the West and the East date back several thousand years, perhaps more than 5000 in the Middle East. The fact that adults learn in different ways than younger people has been intuitively recognized for a long time, and Confucius, Plato and Sir Thomas More all wrote about it. And as an adult that is probably not a surprise to you either.

Organized adult education programs in the West have existed as far back as the 1790s in Britain. In this country, one of the first books on the subject was Eduard Lindeman's *The Meaning of Adult Education,* published in 1926. Thousands of books, studies and learned articles have followed. It is a very popular subject among academics and educators. And although it's still being researched and developed, the fundamentals of the subject are generally agreed upon.

The basic reason we learn differently than younger students is because we are so different from them in so many ways. We've lived longer, and have many more experiences. As we've aged we've acquired more and more responsibilities - a job, perhaps a spouse or partner, maybe some kids, a few bills to be paid and so forth. And with these added responsibilities has come the curse of the last half of the 20th century and the first half of the 21st: less and less time to attend to more and more things that need to be done. So we want to use our time more efficiently.

And overlaying all of these differences is one that is probably more important: we expect to be treated as adults. And that is a concept that many educational systems are still wrestling with in one way or another.

> **"You need to engage the students with hands-on activities, with groups, with field trips. Just lay some stuff out and let them postulate what it might be."**
> *Patrick A., 46, on how to teach adults.*

The way the kids learn

Until the 1930s or so there was only one model used to create curricula, teaching practices and schools. It was the one that was refined from about the 7th to the 12th centuries in the monastic schools of Europe. This model was called *pedagogy*, from the early Greek words meaning child and leading - literally teaching children.

It pictured the mind as a blank slate or an empty container, one that needed to be filled with knowledge about the world and its many aspects. This learning system depended on fact-filled lectures, quizzes, assigned readings, drills, tests, rote memorization and the other techniques you no doubt recall from your days in grammar school and high school.

In the pedagogical model the learner is dependent on the teacher for the transmittal of knowledge, and the student has no control over content or emphasis. He understands that the knowledge he is being given has no real immediate value to him, and he has little real world experience upon which to judge the worth of the knowledge that he is gaining. The whole model assumes that adults, being older, wiser and more experienced, know what is best for the younger learner. The child is told - and generally believes - that what he is being taught today will have some value and relevance in his life later on.

Although this technique works reasonably well for younger students, even with them it has some shortcomings. And it doesn't work at all well for most adults.

> **"We had to write our own plays and perform them in class. That was my favorite kind. It was all hands-on activities."**
> *Deanne L. spent more than twenty years getting her Bachelor's and went on for her Master's.*

Mike Doolin

How we adults learn

Starting in the 1930s, educators and academics began to develop a very different theory about how adults learned. By the 1950s knowledge in the area of adult learning theory was exploding. This was driven by the fact that much of the adult learning that was practiced during those years was failing: the adults were not learning what they were supposed to be learning, and the assumptions that the teachers were using to structure their materials just didn't seem to fit the characteristics of their adult learners.

This new theory of learning developed quickly once the ball got rolling, and by the mid-1960s it had even been given a name: *Andragogy*, a parallel word to pedagogy and based on the Greek word for man or adult. By the 1970s it was clear to most educators that adults did learn differently from younger students, and had, in fact, been learning differently for a very, very long time, even though the formal educational institutions had never recognized these differences.

In a nutshell the differences are these.

• First, adult learners are generally self-directing for the most part. Unlike children, we will take responsibility for what we learn and how and where we learn it.

• Second, because our lives as adults are experience-based, we tend to learn best those things that we experience rather than the ones we just passively hear about in lectures. So the primary methods that are used to successfully teach adults are based on non-lecture techniques such as experiments and other hands-on exercises, group discussions, problem-solving cases, simulations, field studies and other methods that allow us to get our hands dirty, so to speak.

• Third, adult learning is driven by a need to know. It is goal-oriented and concerned with coping with real-life situations or problems.

• And finally, adults want to be able to use their new knowledge quickly, to apply whatever skills or knowledge they've learned today to living more fully and effectively tomorrow.

> "There was more interaction in these classes. It was as if they welcomed debate, they welcomed each student's interpretation, they left room for growth."
> *Kathleen C. started college in 1971. She was 56 when she earned her Bachelor's degree.*

What this means to you
as an adult college student

In the last fifty years or so educators have learned a great deal about how adults learn and how that learning differs from the way young students learn. While some colleges still have not gotten the word, most schools and teachers have incorporated at least some of the theory into the way they offer knowledge to adults. Although you will not see all of these characteristics in every class or every school, you should notice at least some of the basics of andragogical theory at work when you go back to school.

> "....they take everything they know and put it into their lectures. They're not boring. They stimulate you by visual, audio. They take every type of learning and put it into one course. Everybody learns from them.
> *Bette B. on her experience in her local community college.*

Some of the things you might see include:

• Classrooms which look different than you remember. The old style classroom - the one we still use for children in most cases - had the teacher in front of the room and the learners arranged in rows facing her. While this arrangement works OK for children who are dependent on the teacher to transmit knowledge, it doesn't work well for adults, who feel that they should be more in charge of their learning and who don't want to feel subservient to another adult, the teacher.

Consequently, an adult-oriented classroom will often have the learners and the teacher arranged in a circle, or seated around a small collection of tables. Everyone is equal in this space - there is no status differentiation.

The exception to this will probably be classrooms that depend heavily on computers and computer projectors. Many modern classrooms give each student a computer, and the teacher has one as well, with hers driving an overhead projector. These classrooms will probably look a lot like the ones you are familiar with, with the students arranged in rows and the teacher in front of the room. Classrooms that depend on conventional teaching work on blackboards will look familiar as well. Many math classes are still taught like this.

• Better lighting, acoustics and ventilation. We may not want to admit it, but as we age our bodies change, and usually not for the better. Our sight starts to go. By the time we're in our 40s many of us - including this author - are wearing bifocals. It's a fact of life that older eyes just do not see as well as younger ones. The same can be said of our hearing, which is just not as sharp as it is in younger students. And we tend to tire more quickly than when we were in our twenties, so room ventilation is more important for us older folks.

To compensate for some of these conditions, many adult classrooms now include higher light levels, larger type in textbooks, handouts and projected materials like overhead slides, PA systems and generally better acoustic qualities, and increased ventilation.

• A friendly, relaxed atmosphere. Most educators agree that the behavior of the teacher is the single most influential characteristic of the adult learning process. These days, most teachers of adults take the time to get to know their students' names and learn something about them and their individual circumstances. This informal, almost casual environment is made to put everyone at ease.

- Involvement in structuring the course. The adult student's need to be more or less self-directed generates a need for the teacher to allow the student to help plan the course. This usually begins by finding out what the students know in relation to what they should know to master the content of the course, then structuring the course to "fill in the blanks." In this model, the teacher is more of a guide or mentor, helping the students help themselves discover knowledge.
- Use of more "hands-on" learning techniques. Because adults have much more experience than younger students, the way they prefer to learn is much different. Most adults do not like the lecture technique, preferring instead to be more actively involved. Consequently, many adult classes tend to use techniques like role-playing, group discussions, experiments, skill-practice exercises, small seminar and group work activities, team projects and the like. Lectures are still used, but they tend to be much more give and take than the ones you remember from high school, and usually resemble more a group of friends trading knowledge and ideas back and forth.
- Emphasis on practical applications. This is also a reflection of adults' greater experience. Teachers of adults often tie the topic being discussed to a real-life situation where it can be immediately applied. Writing classes, as one example, often have adult students actually write letters of complaint to a retailer they are dissatisfied with, or create a job application letter and resume to send to a potential employer. In many cases these are actually mailed.
- Testing methods emphasize skill competency rather than a regurgitation of "facts." Although tests are still widespread in many courses, there are other ways to measure what students have learned than fill-in-the-blanks and multiple choice tests. Adults are usually motivated to learn because they have specific goals to reach and problems to solve, so more and more testing of adult learners is oriented toward demonstrating specific skills and capabilities.

- The teacher-learner relationship is not based on a rigid hierarchy. Most adults, regardless of their actual learning abilities, are genuinely afraid of returning to school, as noted in an earlier chapter. Schools dealing with adults realize this, and teachers often go to considerable lengths to make the students feel comfortable. A major emphasis is placed on presenting the teacher as a peer, an equal who just happens to have some special knowledge to share. The learning environment often resembles getting information from a friend or mentor.

Not every class, every teacher or every school incorporates all of these new techniques, these revised attitudes. As noted earlier, many institutions are still wrestling with the increasing numbers of adult students showing up in their classrooms and on their rosters. For decades they were charged with cramming knowledge into the heads of 18 year olds. And most of them got pretty good at that.

But now they are faced with students who are, in many cases, older than their faculty. And they are having some difficulties adjusting to this new set of faces.

If you find yourself in a class with a preponderance of adults but the teacher is obviously not using any of the techniques noted above, you may want to ask why. There may be some very good reasons. Or it may be that the instructor is just not aware of the differences in learning styles between adults and younger students.

But don't expect the teacher to instantly adjust her teaching methods - that probably won't happen. About the best you could hope for under these circumstances is that the instructor will take it upon herself to investigate the field of adult learning and eventually incorporate some of the theory into class design.

The Reference section provides information on some excellent beginning books in the field of adult education. You might want to pass those along to any teacher who seems interested.

> "What I loved about it was that you had a chance to become directly involved in the inner workings of your educational program. It was nice, because you could customize it in a way."
> Dave P, commenting on his experience in his non-residential college degree program.

CHAPTER 14

Take This Learning Style Inventory and Get To Know How You Learn

> "And then here, with courses that you take where you have long memorization and midterms, then how do you prepare for that when you haven't done it for 20 years?"
> *Andrea W., 47, took courses in both a traditional 4-year college and a non-traditional school.*

How do <u>you</u> learn?

As we saw in the last chapter, adults learn differently than younger people. But regardless of age, we all learn in different ways, and we respond to information presented to us using different senses. In other words, each of us has a unique learning style.

If we know what our individual learning style is, we can use this information to help tailor our learning environment so that the information we need to learn can be presented to us in the way that is most efficient for us.

The following Learning Styles Inventory can give you some valuable information about how you learn.

For example, some of us learn best by seeing information, some by hearing it, and others by actually experiencing a task. Some of us learn best in groups, while others prefer to be alone. And for some, the best way to report what they've learned is by talking about it, while others prefer to write about it.

Knowing how you learn can help you study more efficiently, and should allow you to do better in classes and on tests. And it should save you time, by allowing you to focus quickly on the best way to learn a particular piece of information.

This inventory will take about 15 - 20 minutes to complete. After you've finished answering all of the questions, read the Description of Learning Style Preferences, then score your answers using the Scoring Sheet. Information on how to interpret your inventory scores follows that.

Note that there are no right or wrong answers. This is not a test in the classic sense; it is only designed to help you determine the best way for you to learn.

> **"My favorite kind of class is one that has discussion. You've got anywhere from 12 to 30 people in the room engaged enough in the topic to have debates, discussions, exchanges of ideas. I love that."**
> *Patrick A. earned his Bachelor's degree in the very late 1990s and went on for his Master's.*

Learning Styles Inventory

OBJECTIVE:
To identify your learning style by giving you a chance to answer a series of statements based on your general reaction to them. Once you answer the statements you'll be able to analyze those answers to learn more about how you learn.

DIRECTIONS:
Read each statement carefully and decide which number, from nine down to one, represents how you feel about that statement. Circle the number which you feel best suits you, i.e. - if the statement is most like you, circle the number 9. If it is like you but not enough to warrant a 9, circle the 7. If it is least like you, circle the number 1; if it is least like you but not enough to warrant a 1, circle the 3. On the rare occasion when you find the statement to be neither like you nor unlike you, circle the five. Answer each of the 45 statements which follow. Take all the time you need.

	Most Like Me			Least Like Me	
1. When I make things while I am learning I remember what I am learning better.	9	7	5	3	1
2. Written assignments are easy for me.	9	7	5	3	1
3. I learn better if someone reads to me than if I read silently to myself.	9	7	5	3	1

	Most Like Me			**Least Like Me**	
4. I get more work done when I work alone.	9	7	5	3	1
5. I remember what I have read better than what I have heard.	9	7	5	3	1
6. When I answer questions, I can say the answer better than I can write it.	9	7	5	3	1
7. When I do math problems in my head, I say the numbers to myself.	9	7	5	3	1
8. If I need help in learning something, I am likely to ask one or more of my fellow learners or someone else for help.	9	7	5	3	1
9. I understand a math problem that is written better than one I hear.	9	7	5	3	1
10. I don't mind doing written assignments.	9	7	5	3	1
11. I find it harder to learn from printed materials than when I am told something.	9	7	5	3	1

	Most Like Me			**Least Like Me**	
12. I like to work by myself.	9	7	5	3	1
13. I would rather read a story than listen to it.	9	7	5	3	1
14. I would rather show and explain how a thing works than write about how it works.	9	7	5	3	1
15. Saying something over and over to remember it works better for me than writing it over and over.	9	7	5	3	1
16. I like to work in a group because I learn from the others.	9	7	5	3	1
17. When the instructor says a number, I really don't understand it until I see it written down.	9	7	5	3	1
18. Writing an item a number of times helps me learn it better.	9	7	5	3	1
19. I find it easier to remember what I have heard than what I have read.	9	7	5	3	1

	Most Like Me			Least Like Me	
20. I learn best when I study alone.	9	7	5	3	1
21. When I have a choice between listening or reading, I usually read.	9	7	5	3	1
22. I feel like I talk smarter than I write.	9	7	5	3	1
23. When I'm told the pages to refer to, I can remember them without writing them down.	9	7	5	3	1
24. I get more work done when I work with one or more other people.	9	7	5	3	1
25. Written math problems are easier for me to solve than spoken ones.	9	7	5	3	1
26. I like to do things with my hands, like simple repairs or manipulating things.	9	7	5	3	1
27. The things I write on paper sound better when I say them.	9	7	5	3	1

	Most Like Me				**Least Like Me**
28. I learn/study best when there is no one around to talk or listen to.	9	7	5	3	1
29. I do well in learning situations where most of the information has to be read.	9	7	5	3	1
30. If learning assignments or homework were oral, I would find it easier to do.	9	7	5	3	1
31. When I have a written math problem to do, I say it to myself to understand it better.	9	7	5	3	1
32. I can learn more about a subject if I am with a small group of learners.	9	7	5	3	1
33. Seeing a number makes more sense to me than hearing a number.	9	7	5	3	1
34. I like to make things with my hands.	9	7	5	3	1
35. I like tests that ask me to complete a sentence or write down the answer.	9	7	5	3	1

	Most Like Me			Least Like Me	
36. I understand more from a group discussion than from reading about a subject.	9	7	5	3	1
37. I learn better by reading than by listening	9	7	5	3	1
38. I would rather tell a story than write it.	9	7	5	3	1
39. It makes it easier to work out a math problem when I say the numbers to myself.	9	7	5	3	1
40. I like to study with other people.	9	7	5	3	1
41. It is easier for me to understand the price of something when it is written down than when it is told to me.	9	7	5	3	1
42. I understand what I have read better when I am involved in making something.	9	7	5	3	1

43. The things I write down on paper sound better than when I talk about them.	9	7	5	3	1
44. I do well on tests if they are about things I hear about.	9	7	5	3	1
45. I think better when I work alone than when I work with someone else.	9	7	5	3	1

We will be determining your score shortly. But first, an explanation of the different learning styles you may have.

DESCRIPTION OF LEARNING STYLE PREFERENCES

The Learning Styles Inventory investigates three main areas involved in most learning projects. These three areas are:

    A.   **Personal Learning Style** - This area is concerned with how you prefer to gather and learn information based on your own personal inclinations.

    B.   **Social Learning Style** - This area is concerned with differentiating whether you like to learn individually, i.e., alone by yourself, or in groups with one or more other individuals.

    C.   **Reporting Learning Style** - This area is concerned with how you best report, express or share what you have learned with others.

Each of the three main areas of learning style is subdivided into two or more learning style preferences. These learning style preferences are outlined below under their main area.

PERSONAL LEARNING STYLES PREFERENCES

    A.   **Visual Language** - People who demonstrate this preference learn best by seeing words in books, on the blackboard, in handouts, on visuals or flipchart pads, in manuals, in workbooks, etc. They tend to write down words they hear in order to learn by seeing them on paper. They remember best, and use, information that they read.

    B.   **Visual Numerical** - People who demonstrate this preference learn best by seeing numbers in order to work with them. They tend to remember and understand math facts if they have seen them. They don't seem to need much oral explanation.

C. **Auditory Language** - People who demonstrate this preference learn best by hearing words spoken. They may vocalize or recite to themselves as they read, particularly when attempting to learn and understand new material. They learn, understand and remember facts they have learned by hearing.

D. **Auditory Numerical** - People who demonstrate this preference learn best from hearing numbers and explanations. They may remember phone numbers, prices, car licenses, etc. with ease, simply by hearing them. They are successful with oral numbers, games and puzzles. They may do just about as well learning something without a manual, book or printed reference as with one, because written materials are not important to them. They probably resolve problems in their heads. They may say numbers to themselves as they read problems.

E. **Auditory-Visual-Kinesthetic Combination** - People who demonstrate this preference learn best through experience. They need a combination of stimuli. The manipulation of material along with the accompanying sight and sounds (words and numbers seen or spoken) make a big difference to their learning. They may not seem to be able to understand assignments, or to be able to keep their minds on their work unless they are totally involved, which includes the physical-manipulative (kinesthetic) part of themselves too. They attempt to, or actually do, handle, touch and work with what they are learning.

SOCIAL LEARNING STYLES PREFERENCES

A. **Individual Learner** - People who demonstrate this preference learn best and get more work done when they learn and work by themselves. They think best, and remember more, when they learn alone. They care more for their own opinions than for the ideas of others. Thinking, learning and remembering are considered solitary experiences.

B. **Group Learner** - People who demonstrate this preference learn best with at least one other person present. They do not get much done studying alone. They value others' opinions and preferences. Group interaction increases their learning and later recognition of facts. Socializing is important to them.

> **"I like lectures, but a lot of people don't. But I'm there to get as much knowledge as I can. So a professor who comes in and lectures, I like."**
> *Karen D. started college in the early 1970s. It took her nearly thirty years to finish her Bachelor's degree. She went on for her Master's.*

REPORTING LEARNING STYLES PREFERENCES

    A.   **Oral Learning Reports** - People who demonstrate this preference can easily tell what they know. They talk fluently and comfortably and seem to be able to say what they mean. They probably know more than their written reports/tests show. They are not shy about giving reports or talking to other people. Organizing and putting thoughts on paper, however, may be difficult for these types of people.

    B.   **Written Learning Reports** - People who demonstrate this preference write reports, technical documents and answers to questions easily. They are uncomfortable giving answers orally. Their thoughts are better organized when written than when given orally.

LEARNING STYLES INVENTORY SCORING SHEET

DIRECTIONS:

    1. Transfer the specific number you circled for each statement in the inventory to the line beside the same statement number below.
    2. Once all blank lines have a number on them, total these numbers for each of the nine style preferences.
    3. Then using the Description of Learning Styles Preferences information and the information below on Interpreting Your Learning Styles Inventory Scores, try to work out a preliminary understanding of how you learn best.

> "I think (independent study) is a natural way to learn. And I believe that it's very beneficial for people who are confident of their abilities."
> *Helen D., 40, worked rotating shifts, making it impossible for her to attend a conventional school. She finished her Bachelor's degree at a non-traditional, non-residential college.*

PERSONAL LEARNING STYLES PREFERENCES

1. **VISUAL LANGUAGE**

   Statement #
   5 _____
   13 _____
   21 _____
   29 _____
   37 _____

   Total _____

2. **VISUAL NUMERICAL**

   9 _____
   17 _____
   25 _____
   33 _____
   41 _____

   Total _____

3. **AUDITORY LANGUAGE**

   3 _____
   11 _____
   19 _____
   36 _____
   44 _____

   Total _____

4. **AUDITORY NUMERICAL**

   7 _____
   15 _____
   23 _____
   31 _____
   39 _____

   Total _____

5. **AUDITORY-VISUAL KINESTHETIC COMBINATION**

   1 _____
   18 _____
   26 _____
   34 _____
   42 _____

   Total _____

SOCIAL LEARNING STYLES PREFERENCE(S)

6. **INDIVIDUAL LEARNER** 7. **GROUP LEARNER**

    4 _____   8 _____
   12 _____   16 _____
   20 _____   24 _____
   28 _____   32 _____
   45 _____   40 _____

Total _____ Total _____

REPORTING LEARNING STYLES PREFERENCE(S)

8. **ORAL EXPRESSIVENESS** 9. **WRITTEN EXPRESSIVENESS**

    6 _____   2 _____
   14 _____   10 _____
   22 _____   27 _____
   30 _____   35 _____
   38 _____   43 _____

Total _____ Total _____

INTERPRETING YOUR LEARNING STYLES INVENTORY SCORES

The learning styles inventory can be divided into three main styles areas:
1. Personal learning styles –
preferences 1 to 5 on the scoring sheet.
2. Social learning styles –
preferences 6 and 7 on the scoring sheet.
3. Reporting learning styles –
preferences 8 and 9 on the scoring sheet.

In assessing your style of learning based on this inventory, you should look for your highest score in each of the three main areas. Each of these areas gives you varying information about your personal learning styles. Using this information may prove helpful in trying to adapt learning environments to best suit your personal learning style.

You should find some score variation between various learning style preferences. The highest scoring item is obviously the dominant or major learning style preference you have for the area you are considering. If two or three other scores are close to your highest scoring preference, interpret this to mean that you are comfortable using more than one particular learning pattern, and therefore have greater variety in the various approaches to learning that you can use.

Scores in any of the nine preference areas can range from a high of 45, indicating a style in which you find learning very easy, to a low of 5, indicating a style in which you will have extreme difficulty learning anything.

Scores 36 and Above

Scores in this range represent your Dominant learning style(s). Given a learning situation where you can use your own natural learning pattern(s), you will use this/these styles.

Scores Between 26 and 35

Scores in this range represent your Major learning style(s) preference(s), indicating learning modes in which you should find yourself very comfortable using in learning new things, even if they are not a "natural" style for you.

Scores Between 16 and 25

Scores in this range represent your Minor learning style(s) preference(s). You can learn using these minor styles, but they will be your second choice if you have a chance to use a Major preference. You can use these minor learning styles alone, but you are more likely to use them in combination with your major preference(s).

Scores Between 5 and 15

Scores in this range represent learning preferences of Negligible Usefulness to you in trying to learn new things. Trying to learn using these style preferences should make learning difficult and uncomfortable for you personally.

Once you've determined your major style preferences, you may want to review the description of those learning style preferences. This should help clear up and focus your understanding of just what is involved in the main learning style preferences you have identified about yourself.

Knowing more about your personal learning style preferences should help you:

1. Understand yourself better
2. Organize and plan personal learning endeavors better
3. Adjust learning situations where you are a participant under the direction of another person such as an instructor.

NOTE: Maybe you'd like to compare your learning style preferences to mine. Here are my scores:

1. Visual Language:	37
2. Visual Numerical	35
3. Auditory Language	21
4. Auditory Numerical	25
5. Auditory-Visual-Kinesthetic Comb.	39
6. Individual Learner	39
7. Group Learner	25
8. Expressiveness - Oral	11
9. Expressiveness - Written	41

This Learning Styles Inventory has been adapted slightly from Knaak, W. C. (1983). *Learning styles: Applications in vocational education.* (Information series No. 254). Columbus, OH: The National Center for Research in Vocational Education. This is ERIC Document # ED 229 573. You can get more information about this Learning Styles Inventory at the Education Resources Information Center at http://www.eric.ed.gov:80/ERICWebPortal/Home.portal?_nfpb=true&ERICExtSearch_SearchValue_0=Knaak&ERICExtSearch_SearchType_0=au&_pageLabel=RecordDetails&objectId=0900000b80112cef

Entering Learning Styles Inventory into an internet search engine will give you dozens of similar questionnaires, and many of these will be considerably shorter.

> **"(she was) my ideal teacher. There was always encouragement, interaction, always asking the right questions to make the students feel smart. She's the first one who made me think, gee, maybe I can do this."**
>
> *Ann H. reflecting on one of her first teachers in the community college she attended. Ann went on for her Master's Degree.*

CHAPTER 15

Start Slow, Start Smart

> "But when you get that first A on a paper you say, I can do this. I can build on what I did with this paper.... and I can probably go on from there to do anything I want to. Each semester I tend to set my goals a little higher as far as my grades are concerned."
>
> *Linda W., 41, started at her local community college in the very late 1970s and earned her Associate's degree about 20 years later. She earned her Bachelor's degree a few years after that.*

Go slow at first until you figure it out

If you've been away from organized learning for any length of time, say since high school, getting back into the classroom is going to be a shock to your nervous system. You'll be sitting still for hours on end, and listening to someone who might be less than captivating (this is not MTV or prime-time television). You'll be asked to concentrate on material that might seem slightly mysterious at best, boring at worst. And you'll be responsible for turning in assignments and researching papers, etc.

Recommendation:
Take just one course

And make it a course on a subject that you are interested in. If you have some background in the material, that's even better.

What you're trying to do here is build up your self-esteem and confidence. College is <u>not</u> that hard. There are more than 7.5 million adult students sitting in classes and taking courses as you read this. Many millions more have successfully completed college while still working, tending to a family, having something of a social life and shouldering all the rest of the responsibilities of being an adult.

But you probably don't believe that you could duplicate that success. You are probably - if you are honest with yourself - terrified of the prospect of going back to school.

And that's fine. You probably wouldn't be normal if you weren't at least a little apprehensive. This book and others like it can try to encourage you and give you a roadmap to make your transition back into school a bit easier. But we all know better than to think that a book is going to completely convince you that you can do this. The only one who can do that for you is you.

So the standard advice from everyone connected with returning adult students is this: start slow. Take <u>one</u> course. A course where you have a very high probability of succeeding. One that will be interesting, relatively easy to do the work in. And fun! That's very important, at least for this first class. You've got to be able to enjoy this first experience.

If you were lousy in high school math, an advanced calculus class is probably not a good place to start. Taking a course that you have a good chance of failing is not going to do much for your ego or your self-confidence.

And you're also trying to ease slowly into a very alien system, one that is, in many cases, specifically designed to accommodate 18-year olds. Not you. College has, in many ways, a different set of rules and conventions than the adult world you are used to inhabiting.

If you were somehow plunked down into the middle of a foreign country, you would expect that it would take you awhile to get used to your new surroundings, to get acquainted with the new culture, to learn to speak the new language. The same is true of returning to school. It takes some getting used to. Taking a single, fun, interesting class can make that adjustment a lot easier.

> **"Just have confidence in yourself, take it slow, and roll with the punches."**
> *Ann H., 33, started at her community college in the early 1990s. She ultimately earned her Bachelor's degree and went on for her Master's.*

A few hints about what to look for in your first class

Some types of classes will be better than others as starter classes. For instance, courses that run during regular length semesters will probably be a bit easier to handle, at least for the neophyte student. A 15-week course meets about three hours a week, or roughly 45 hours of total class time. The same course in a 6-week summer semester will give you about an eight-hour-a-week class that still has to cover the same material and will require you to do the same amount of work in about one third the time.

You can see the problem. This acceleration is hard enough to cope with if you are an experienced student. Don't set yourself up to fail by taking a condensed class right away. They just move too quickly.

Classes that are reading or writing intensive are tougher for some learners than those that are not writing intensive. How can you tell which is which? Most schools give writing-intensive courses a special code. Lacking that, check with an adviser. Better yet, ask someone in the department that offers the class.

Reading-intensive classes will probably require you to buy a ton of books. Go to the bookstore and check on the books required for the class you are interested in. If it requires half a dozen 400 page books, it's probably something you want to avoid as a first class.

Also try to make your first class one that will count toward your degree. There's no point in wasting this time and money if you can get it to count. Almost all the entry-level, "101" type classes can be used to fulfill degree requirements. These are often tagged with words like "Introduction to", "Beginning", "Basic", "Elementary", etc. English, Psychology, Math, Biology, Chemistry, Physics, Physical Education, Sociology, and History are some of the courses you are likely to find in this category.

As an aside, Introductory courses tend to be just that. They are introductions to the material, a survey of the field. They give you a little taste of everything in the subject. They are usually very broad-brush, and cover a lot of material but none of it in any real depth. And they are specifically targeted at beginners. They are generally 100-level classes, which means they are Freshman courses. And Freshmen, of course, are the beginners in college.

An Intro to Literature course, as an example, will probably expose you to fiction, poetry, drama, maybe some biographies, some non-fiction, perhaps even a movie. You'll learn to recognize the various forms of literature and get exposed to some of the well-known authors and poets. But you won't learn about any of these subjects in any great detail.

Courses that you have some background in are also excellent candidates for starter classes, but be aware that these may <u>not</u> count toward your degree. If you have always enjoyed working on your own car, for example, an Introduction to Automotive Technology class might be a good, fun, interesting choice. Maybe your hobby is decorating your home. If so, Beginning Interior Design would be a good place to start.

Another strategy is to take a course in a subject that has always interested you but you never had the time to learn more about it. Maybe that trip to Mexico triggered an interest in learning Spanish, or discovering more about the Maya or Aztecs. Perhaps your general suspicion of advertising could lead to taking an Introduction to Mass Media class. If you've always been fascinated with personal computers or web site design, there are probably classes designed to give you more information in an easy-to-digest format.

The point is to get started in a class where you will <u>succeed</u>. Some school, college, business or organization in your town is offering a class that could easily be the start of your college career. That class will be fun and interesting. The work will be fairly straightforward, and the instructor will work with you to help you get over your apprehension and see that you succeed.

> **"There's no such thing as failing except if you do not try. So if you want to get into school and you don't because you're afraid, then you fail."**
> *Bette B., 40 and the mother of two teenagers, worked 23 hours a week, went to school full time, and carried a 4.0 GPA. She earned her Associate's degree, then her Bachelor's. She has plans for a Master's.*

CHAPTER 16

Chopping That 120 Credit Hour Goal Down To Manageable Size: Not All Of Your Credits Have To Come From The Classroom

> "I've volunteered for so many organizations and done so much stuff with my life that I was able to sit down (with my mentor) and justify 48 credits. And I didn't take any CLEP tests. That's all life experience."
> *Rich B., 44, married with six children, fell off a scaffold and became disabled. He enrolled at his non-traditional, non-residential four year college and earned a Bachelor's Degree in just 2-1/2 years.*

There are lots of ways to earn credit!

When the 18-year-old day-school kids sign up to go to college, virtually all of them can expect to sit through all 40+ classes that it typically takes to get a 4-year Bachelor's degree. They are young, inexperienced, probably have never had a full-time job, and almost certainly are not married and don't have children.

Only some of the college experience for these people is designed to instill knowledge of a particular subject. Much of it is meant to help them grow up and mature, to teach them responsibility, to learn how to work together in groups, and to generally socialize them so that down the road somewhere they can become productive members of society.

While you may not have anyone footing the bill for you to go to school like many of the kids do, you do have a lot of advantages that they do not have. As a fully-functioning, older, experienced, employed adult who has already assumed a lot of responsibilities in his or her life, you have already learned most of the things that the kids have yet to learn. And you did it just by showing up for life.

And guess what? You could very well turn some - perhaps a lot - of this experience into class credits...without <u>ever</u> having to sit through a particular class.

I'll say that again:

You may not have to actually attend a class to get credit for it!

In fact, you might be able to get credit for as many as a dozen or more of your required 40-some classes, just by demonstrating what you already know.

And while you might actually enjoy sitting in the classroom for those classes, taking them is definitely going to slow you down in your quest for that piece of paper. If your goal is to just get that degree and get on with your life, read this section carefully. *You might be able to eliminate several years of part-time school!*

There are a variety of ways to get college credit, and attending classes in person is only one of them.

While every school is of course different, most schools will allow most of the techniques discussed below. You'll want to check with the advising and admissions folks at your school on the specifics, but let's look at some possibilities.

CLEP Tests

The College Level Examination Program (CLEP) has been developed by the College Entrance Examination Board (http://www.collegeboard.com/?student). These $55 tests measure general educational knowledge and understanding of basic facts and principles.

CLEP is a national system of credit by examination that is available through nearly every accredited two-year and four-year college. According to the College Board, there are 2,900 colleges that grant credit and/or advanced standing for CLEP exams.

There are at least several dozen of these exams, with subjects ranging from general exams in English, College Math, the Humanities, and Social Sciences and History, to French, German and Spanish, to History, Government, Economics, Psychology and Sociology, to Math including Calculus, Trig and Algebra, sciences such as Biology and Chemistry, and various business subjects such as Management, Accounting and Marketing. Here is the most up-to-date list: http://www.collegeboard.com/student/testing/clep/exams.html

How much credit can you earn with the CLEP tests? A lot. It is entirely possible that you could test out of a year or more of college, just by successfully taking these tests. As an example, someone who has a good grasp of one of the foreign languages noted above could pick up as many as 12 credit hours from a single exam. Passing the Introductory Accounting exam would net you 8 hours. Passing the general exam in English would pass you out of both English 101 (Composition) plus an English elective in most schools - six hours of credit.

Most of the CLEP tests are 90-minutes long, and comprised mostly of multiple-choice questions. Most of the English tests include writing, and language tests include reading, writing and speaking. Most schools offer these tests on a regular basis, but since they are nationally recognized, you can take them in one school and easily transfer them into any other.

In addition to the CLEP tests, states often have their own credit by test systems.

Your school's registration department should have information on CLEP. Your adviser should certainly have complete information on this subject. If he doesn't know how you might be able to get information on CLEP, you might want to find another adviser.

For a recap of this program, visit the College Board's CLEP site at http://www.collegeboard.com/student/testing/clep/about.html

> **"I got credit for military experience. (They) filled up my general electives and my physical education. I got a total of 31 credits."**
> *Joyce M., 36 and the single mother of three kids, worked 20 hours a week at her community college and carried a full time class load. She earned her Associate's with a 3.8 GPA. She's on track to earn a Master's.*

Departmental tests

In addition to CLEP, which nearly all accredited schools will accept, many schools offer you the ability to test out of various subjects like English 101, Writing, History, Introductory Math, the beginning Sciences, etc. These programs are created and run within given departments in the school, using their own departmental tests. Exams in more advanced subjects might also be available. Check with your adviser.

Your job

Yes, believe it or not, you may well be able to get college credit simply for being a grown up and holding down a job! This is especially true if your job is in your major field. Once again, check with your adviser. If your school has someone in charge of Experiential Learning, go to them.

Military experience

College-level courses are widely available through all branches of the U.S. Military services. Formerly called the United States Armed Forces Institute (USAFI), the program is now called DANTES, the Defense Activity for Non-Traditional Education Support.

Training that you received while in the military might be transferable to your college. This training might include (but not be limited to) tech schools and leadership courses.

In many schools military service will also substitute for the required physical education courses. Since many schools don't offer a lot of phys ed classes at night or on weekends when most adult students are actually available to take those classes, this can be very helpful.

If you were in the military - active or reserve - and took any training at all, in anything, it will pay to review those courses with the registration and advisement people at your school. If this training has been evaluated by the American Council on Education (http://www.acenet.edu), it may translate into college credit.

To get copies of your military training records, refer to the Reference section for the address to write to. Your local recruiting office may also be able to help you, although they will probably just send you to the address in the Reference section. Many colleges also have a Veteran's Affairs person on staff – they will know how to access your military training records and have them evaluated for college credit. Be warned that this process might take a couple of months start to finish. If you think you'll need this information, start the process now.

And if you can't find your DD-214 Discharge papers, get a copy of that as well, since you will almost certainly need it. Again, your school's Veteran's Affairs person should be able to help.

> "I expect to be getting credit for my life experiences - my stationary engineering licenses, my pesticide certification, the computer courses I've taken through (work), my refrigeration licenses. I'll probably get around 15 hours."
> *Helen D., 40 and the single mother of one child, kept at it for nearly 25 years to get her Bachelor's degree.*

Life experience:
credit by evaluation

Many schools award credits for what they like to call experiential learning, the experiences you have had as an adult. These programs go by various names, including Credit By Evaluation and Portfolio Assessment or Portfolio Development. Whatever your school calls it, I call it showing up for life, because that's what it amounts to. Credit possibilities include work experience, volunteer service, conferences, workshops, in-service training, professional licenses, hobbies, certifications awarded from professional organizations, independent readings, even travel.

That trip to Mexico you took a few years ago to help an anthropologist on a Mayan dig might be worth some hours. Those company-sponsored crash courses in Total Quality Management might have some already-earned credit hours lurking in them. The fact that you are already an electronics repair tech for your company might be enough to get you out of those basic electronics courses you need for your engineering degree. Your Amateur Radio (Ham) license or Private Pilot's license might also deliver some credit to your transcript. EMT certificates, insurance licenses, real estate and brokerage licenses, certification as an alcohol or child development counselor - all might well be accepted for some type of credit. The fact that you were raised in a bi-lingual household and read, write and speak another language is probably good for some foreign language credits. And your hobby of reading science fiction or Victorian romances might be a credit-worthy substitute for your Literature class requirement.

There are a lot of other possibilities in this "get credit for living" category. Talk it over with your registration office people or adviser. You might be pleasantly surprised.

> **"(My college) accepted the Paralegal course as one full semester. So, looking at the cost, I saved pretty close to $2000 with their having given me credit for that certification."**
> *Kathleen C., 56 and the mother of three grown children, went to college for nearly 30 years to earn her Bachelor's degree.*

Televised classes

If you have a local TV channel, a cable system or a Public Broadcasting System channel in your city, you have the first requirement for a televised course: some way to televise it. Many colleges conduct one or more classes live, on the air, every semester.

How these classes work varies by school, but in general you register for these classes just as you would any other course, buy a book, do papers and homework assignments and mail or email them to the instructor, who grades them and gets them back to you. At the end of the course you get credit for the class, just as if you were sitting in a classroom.

Another variant has you watching TV every other class, or every third class, with the no-TV classes spent on campus in a conventional classroom.

And with the widespread availability of VCRs, DVD recorders and TIVO devices, you can effectively be in two places at once, by recording the televised class and replaying it at a more convenient time.

> "(This televised course) saves me a lot of time. It (only) meets five times in the classroom. This could be a class that meets twice a week, but I'm only coming in five times. Then on Thursday morning I watch TV. I get a kick out of it because I'm sitting there in my pajamas basically sitting in class. I get up, get a bowl of cereal, sit down and write down all my notes. And I'm all set."
> *Jason B. commenting on his televised course.*

Video classes

This is another possibility you'll want to investigate. Many schools have taped an entire semester of a particular class, and those tapes are in the school library. Ask your librarian if your school has any of these. Then ask the heads of the departments that taped the classes if a particular course is available for credit by viewing the videotapes and doing the class assignments.

These classes are sometimes listed in the schedule, but in many cases you are going to have to do some digging to find them.

Correspondence classes

Some classes are already structured as correspondence classes, with syllabus, book requirements, homework assignments, tests and everything else you need all assembled in a single box or envelope. Once again, these classes may not show up in the course schedule. Ask some questions of various department heads, or check with your adviser.

Independent study

Many schools will allow you to custom-construct a class for credit in a particular subject area. You usually work with a teacher, the class involves a significant amount of outside reading or studying, and you normally have to turn in a final project - a research paper, a musical composition, a film, a short story, a piece of art, etc. The schedule is usually mutually agreed upon between you and the person who supervises it, and could run from a few weeks to an entire semester or longer.

You may already be working on some project as a part of your job or hobby that might qualify for an independent study course. Since you already have a very good handle on the subject matter, you might be able to crash through the necessary independent study requirements in just a few weeks - a much better way to earn credit than sitting through four months of classes!

I personally used most of these methods on my journey to a college education. As one example, I received full credit for a required Advertising course just by turning in copies of the two product catalogs I was already writing as a part of my full-time day job.

Bang! Three credits!

I got through a required Advertising Media course by taking a short test and turning in copies of the magazine advertising schedules I was already creating as a part of my employment.

Bang! Another three credits!

Don't fool yourself into believing this is an <u>easy</u> way to get credit. It's not. Independent study can be a fair amount of work. It is easy only in the sense that you get to pick the subject and the schedule for doing the work. But it is certainly another viable option in your quest for college credit and that all-important piece of paper.

The non-traditional college

In 1971, the State University of New York launched Empire State College, its "college without a campus." This non-traditional, non-residential college was based on the idea that students would work one-on-one with a mentor, someone who would guide them through a given course of independent study. A series of these studies, called contracts, would, taken together, constitute a degree: an Associate's, a Bachelor's or a Master's degree.

Empire State College (www.suny.esc.edu) was among the first schools to attempt this innovative delivery method. Most of the rest of them have since failed. But Empire State, as a part of one of the largest university systems in the world – the State University of New York – had the resources to work out the inevitable early bugs. It has become the most successful of its kind by far. It was the first public, non-traditional college in the United States to be accredited by the Middle States Association, the same organization that accredits the State University of New York system. At any given moment Empire State has something in excess of 10,000 students, and can boast nearly 50,000 graduates in its nearly thirty year history.

Empire State - and the handful of schools which use a similar model - offer yet another way for the adult student to pursue a degree. These non-traditional, non-residential colleges have no campuses, no classrooms. Student and mentor - in ESC's case usually a PhD - jointly construct a course of study in a subject, specifying what is to be learned, and how that learning will be measured. The student goes off to read the materials they have decided on, checking back in every week or two with his mentor to discuss issues, progress and questions.

At the end of the study, usually a semester in length, the student must demonstrate that he has, indeed, mastered the materials they have agreed upon.

Note that courses pursued in a non-traditional setting tend to be very heavy in reading and writing. Since there is no classroom attendance, and in many cases no tests, the professor has no day-to-day gauge of how well a student is doing. The student has to demonstrate a thorough understanding of the material, and this is usually done through papers.

Empire State and the few schools like it also have the ability to deliver course work through distance learning, providing yet another set of options.

And their systems make it relatively simple (not easy, just simple) to get credit for prior learning. More than four out of five Empire State Bachelor's students, for example, get credit by evaluation, and the average student earns about 34 credits in this fashion. That's a full year's worth of credit toward a Bachelor's degree.

> **"I picked (my non-traditional college) for the flexibility of not sitting in the classroom for several hours a week. Even if money were no object, I'd pick the same type of program again."**
>
> *Andrea W., 47, employed full time and the single mother of one child, started at a community college in the late 1960s and finally finished her Bachelor's Degree more than thirty years later.*

Most day school students don't have a clue that these sorts of credit possibilities even exist. That's no surprise, since most day school students have not really had much in the way of life experiences - they have just not been around all that long. So many schools mention these alternate credit-earning possibilities only briefly somewhere in their catalog.

You will probably have to do a little digging to find out what options are available at your school. Start with the registration/ admissions office. Talk to your advisers. You might want to check in with the heads of the various departments in your school.

But all that research will probably be worth it. You may be very surprised at the wide variety of options available, and at how much credit you can actually amass through these non-classroom modes of learning.

Note that just because you can get credit for a class without actually attending it, doesn't mean that you won't have to pay for it. You almost certainly will have to pay for the class. It may be a per-credit charge, it may be a fee to take a test, it might be a charge to set up and monitor a special project. But you are probably going to have to pay something to get that credit.

These non-classroom-based modes can offer great flexibility for the busy, time-frenzied adult student. Some of these courses can be completed in a matter of weeks or less. Some offer the possibility of no course work whatsoever, just the completion of forms or the taking of a short test. The beauty of these techniques is that several can be combined. Take a few CLEP tests, earn some credit by evaluation, scout up some departmental tests, log onto the net for a course or two, then maybe check out one of the non-traditional, non-residential colleges in the country. A few weeks or months of concentrated activity on your part may yield a bonanza of credit. It's certainly worth looking into.

"The first thing they ask is, can I do it? The self-confidence issue. I've been out of school for 20 years. They don't realize that although they've been dormant in a sense, boy!, their minds are sharp! They're focused, they're goal-oriented, they're motivated. And once they get past the idea that they can't do it, and they find out they can do it - watch out! All you can see is their smoke!"
Bill Sigismond is the Director of Experiential and Adult Learning at Monroe Community College in Rochester, NY.

CHAPTER 17

Online Learning

> "(My Internet class) was great! Actually, if I would have sat down, I probably could have done the whole class in one week, because it was all laid out for you. Everything was mapped out."
> *Jason B. talking about his web-based Coaching Theories class.*

Going to school without going to class!

If you're thinking of returning to college, or perhaps already made the jump, you hear the term online learning a lot. You may be moderately familiar with its meaning, or you may not know anything about it. We'll take a closer look at this relatively new form of learning here. By the end of this chapter you may be able to determine if online learning can help you in your quest for that piece of paper.

What is online learning?
What does the term mean?
Simply, online learning is learning via the internet; you are 'online.' You "attend" class by sitting in front of your computer and interacting with various parts of a web site – probably in the comforts of your own home. This method of learning is becoming wildly popular, for a lot of very good reasons. But like all things, it has both benefits and disadvantages, and we'll take a look at both in this chapter.

On line learning is the natural successor to the correspondence classes of yesterday (although those are still around here and there). But now there's no waiting for the mail to arrive to get your next lesson or to find out how you did on that last assignment. Everything travels at the speed of light. And for certain kinds of students, this kind of learning is making the trip to that degree a whole lot easier.

Who should be interested in online classes?
While nearly anyone can benefit from online classes, certain kinds of students are likely to get the most from them:

• Students who need scheduling flexibility
• Students who live some distance from a physical campus
• Students whose health or other circumstances make it difficult or impossible to attend classes in person

One of the biggest benefits to attending classes online is that you attend on your schedule, not the school's. For folks who work rotating shifts, whose work schedule changes every few weeks, who travel regularly, or who have to stay home to tend to small children or other family members, this is obviously a good solution. You can log in to your class whenever it is convenient for you, even if that's in the middle of the night or you are halfway around the world.

For people who have some difficulty getting to a physical campus, either because of distance, health concerns, or some other circumstance, online classes are a godsend. You no longer have to choose between long distance drives or giving up on your dream of an education. If you have access to a computer and the internet, classes are as close as your keyboard.

Specific Benefits of Online Learning
• **Operate on your own schedule**
• **No physical classes to attend**

What are the disadvantages?
Although online classes have some powerful attractions, they are not for everyone. Lots of people who enroll in online classes either fail them or never complete them. And some of the reasons for this poor completion rate aren't all that obvious.

All successful online students have one characteristic in common: a very high level of motivation. While most adult students already have excellent motivation – they are in college as busy adults, after all – the sort of motivation involved in online learning is somewhat different.

Since you are operating on your own schedule, not the school's, you have to figure out what that schedule is going to be. And stick to it. There is no teacher reminding you show up every Thursday at 6 PM. Or that you have to log in to your class to engage in a discussion or read an assignment. You have to schedule yourself. Some students just can't figure out how to stay on a schedule without the prompt of regular attendance in a physical class. If you're one of them, an online class may not be the right solution for you.

It's not immediately obvious, but online classes typically take more time than classroom based classes, up to 20% to 30% more time by some estimates. A lot of this extra time is because these classes move at the speed of typing, not voice. Things like class discussions, in particular, happen at a much more leisurely pace. And you have to spend more time online to get the benefits of these discussions.

You recapture some of this extra time spent by not having to drive to the campus, but likely not all of it. You can count on online classes taking more time to do. If you can't afford to spend a little extra time for one of these classes, it may not be the right choice for you.

For many students, part of the fun of going to college is the socializing you get to do in class, both with your fellow classmates and with your teacher. You won't get any of this online. Your online class could well be made up of students from all over the country, if not all over the world. You are not likely to ever meet any of them. Ditto for your teacher, who in many cases might be conducting her class out of her home office. If that social interaction is important to you, you won't get it in an online environment.

Specific disadvantages of online learning:
- **High levels of motivation required**
- **More time required**
- **Lack of socializing**

**If you are a new college student,
you may want to wait before trying an online class**

Many educators don't recommend online classes for beginning college students. This author is among them. Why? Because brand new adult students already have their hands full, trying to get back into the learning mode, trying to juggle a new and major time commitment and stuff it into their already packed schedules. Adding the complexities of an online class to this mix just complicates the student's life even more. Many of us tell new adult students to get a semester of classroom classes under their belt first, then add online classes. While this isn't always possible, it is recommended.

How does an online class actually work?

Although every school is different, most online classes are structured similarly. Here's a typical scenario.

When you register for an online class, either in person at your school, or over the internet, you will probably be asked to attend a short seminar. If you are within driving distance to your school, this workshop will probably be on campus. If your school is some distance away, you may be asked to show up at a website at a certain date and time. Or they may send you a CD that walks you through the process. However you attend this preliminary class, it will familiarize you with how to access the class, and how to navigate around the site that your class is on. You will likely be issued a password to allow you to access the site.

Most classes have an index or home page that carries the site map and other navigational cues. If you can use the worldwide web, you will find online learning very familiar. From your class home page you will be able to go to parts of your electronic "classroom" to pick up or deliver assignments, engage in class discussions, visit one on one with your instructor, take tests, read short lectures etc. Everything that you would be able to do in a conventional classroom will be mirrored in this web-based class. The only exceptions to this are hands-on lab work. And a lot of very smart people are working hard on that problem.

Behind the scenes, your instructor is doing everything she would normally do in a classroom, except that she – like you – is operating electronically. She's posting assignments, reading homework, giving and grading tests, engaging in and initiating classroom discussions. And while you are not aware of it, she is also doing a few other things, like monitoring your attendance patterns, the amount of time you spend in various parts of your "classroom," and your interaction with her and with others in your class.

This behind the scenes activity on the part of the instructor can cause problems, mostly for younger, less responsible students. Sometimes students come to the erroneous conclusion that because they are not physically in a classroom that no one actually knows whether they show up or not.

Not true. The software that drives most online classes also monitors the comings and goings of everyone who logs in and out. With a couple of mouse clicks the teacher can instantly determine which students checked in, when they checked in, what parts of the site they spent their time in, how much time they spent in each area and in total, and what they did. Did John get his paper in on time? Has Suzy participated in class discussions? Which ones? What did she have to offer to the class? In seconds your teacher can answer these and many other questions about who is doing what. And just as in a physical classroom, your behavior, level of contributions and quality of work will affect your final grade.

Make sure the online school is accredited

As mentioned elsewhere in this book, accreditation is a process of review by an independent, outside organization. This very in-depth review is conducted every few years, usually takes some months to complete, and insures that the school has the capability to deliver what it promises, that it is staffed with qualified educators, that it has a concrete program of study, and that it is financially sound.

Just as legitimate colleges with a physical presence are accredited by one of the large, national accreditation agencies, so too are online schools. But because online schools may not actually have a physical presence, it can be much easier to create an online college. There are no buildings full of classrooms to put up, no labs to furnish. Offices can be as simple as a computer and an internet connection.

It's not hard to imagine that some people might view this ease of entry into the world of college education as an easy way to make some money quickly. And that is exactly what has happened in some cases. A few computers, a couple of flashy brochures, some concentrated advertising on web sites likely to attract potential adult students and voila! You have an online university!

Except that its purpose is not to provide an education. These "colleges" are designed only to extract money from unsuspecting students. You might wind up with a "degree." But it literally won't be worth the paper it's printed on. And no one will accept it as a legitimate college education.

There have been a number of articles published recently about scam online schools. Go here for a short list of these articles: http://aolsearch.aol.com/aol/search?query=scam+online+schools&invocationType=rl&=AOL+Search

How to check accreditation

To check the accreditation of any college or university, visit the Council for Higher Education Accreditation's (CHEA) database at www.chea.org or call them at 202-234-5100. Internationally based schools are best checked by contacting the host country's Ministry of Education.

Here is a link to the list of the major regional accreditation agencies. If your school is not accredited by one of these organizations, you may want to do a bit more research on that school before you begin to take classes there (and give them your money.)
http://www.chea.org/Directories/regional.asp

What to look for in an online school

Is the online school you are considering a legitimate one, capable of offering a degree that will be accepted and valued by you and others? You'll have to do a little research. Here are a few questions to ask.

- Is the school accredited by one of the national agencies?
- What other schools are also accredited by this agency?
- What are the admission requirements? Are they similar to other legitimate schools? If it seems like they will take anyone with a pulse and a checkbook, beware.
- What - exactly – do you have to do to earn the degree? If large amounts of credit are being offered for "life experience," be wary.
- How quickly can you earn this degree? Anyone advertising a degree in weeks or months is almost certainly not legitimate.
- Is this online school a part of a larger college or university that has campuses and other physical facilities? Virtually all major state university systems and many private schools offer online classes in addition to their campus offerings.
- Will these online credits transfer into another school?
- How long has this online school been in business?
- How accepted are their degrees, especially in the major that you are pursuing?
- What do businesses think about this college and its degrees?
- Would this degree be accepted if you wanted to get into grad school somewhere else? Here's an interesting Business Week magazine article about MBA programs online: http://www.businessweek.com/bschools/content/aug2005/bs2005 0818_4192_bs001.htm

The bottom line on online learning
- Determine if this mode of learning is right for you and your present circumstances
- Make sure the online school you use is accredited
- Make sure your online credits will transfer if you will be completing your degree somewhere else
- Make sure your online degree will be accepted if you are going on to grad school

Other resources
Where do you find Internet classes? Not surprisingly, one of the best places to start your search is on the Internet itself. Keywords like Distance Education, Distance Learning, Online Learning or Lifelong Learning entered into one of the major search engines will return literally thousands of possible sites. In addition to those specific schools listed above, here are several sites to get you started:

http://www.onlinecollegedegrees.net/ This is an extensive listing of schools offering online degrees.

http://www.nova.edu - this is the home page for Nova University, and provides information about Nova's programs and links to other similar sites. Nova is a pioneer in distance learning education.

http://www.phoenix.edu/ This is the home page for the University of Phoenix, the nation's largest online university. It offers Bachelor's, Master's and Doctoral programs.

http://www.esc.edu/esconline/online2.nsf/eschome?openform - this is the home page for Empire State College, a unit of the State University of New York. ESC was one of the first colleges in the world to offer non-traditional education, and was the first accredited university to do so in this country.

http://sln.suny.edu/sln – this is the home page for the State University of NY online learning campus. Offering more than 2000 classes, it is one of the largest providers of online classes in the world.

http://www.petersons.com - this is the home page for Peterson's Publishing, generally regarded as the premier publisher of information about colleges.

In addition to these web sites, Peterson's Guide to Distance Learning Programs offers detailed descriptions of hundreds of institutions offering some form of distance learning. Nearly all of them provide web-based instruction.

> "I'm looking forward to taking another (Internet class). You can't beat it. You get to sit home in your pajamas on your own schedule."
> *Jason B. used an on-line class to plug a hole in his schedule.*

CHAPTER 18

What About Those Classes That I Absolutely Have To Take But Aren't Offered When And How I Need Them?

> "As luck would have it, the first three courses that I would have to take were core courses, only offered in the daytime. So I approached my boss and said, is it possible for me to rearrange my schedule. .... And once again she said, I told you before, it's a choice between your job and your education."
> *Kathleen C., 56, commenting on the trials of getting a degree completely through night school.*

Occasionally, detailed planning just doesn't work

If you've planned well, and the gods of adult students are smiling on you, all of the courses and credits you need to accumulate for your degree will fall into place exactly as they should, right on schedule, when and where and how you expect them.

As noted in an earlier chapter, this won't happen automatically: with hundreds or maybe thousands of courses offered in a given school, and so many different ways to get credit, there are many possibilities for error in schedule planning. You need to hook up early on with an adviser who is used to working with adult students and their non-traditional needs, and the two of you need to create - on paper - a course schedule that can be followed from semester to semester.

If you do this, the chances are very great that you won't need any of the advice in this chapter. Everything will happen as you anticipate, and you will never find yourself scrambling to fill an unexpected hole in your schedule.

But....it could happen. A professor who was the only one who ever taught the course you need retires or moves on. A department is reorganized and your needed course gets lost in the shuffle. The Curriculum Committee comes up with a new version of your major, and the course plan you've been working with is no longer applicable. (This should not affect most students. Most schools will "grandfather" you in on the old curriculum. If they don't, holler! You may have to ask.) Or the course is still available, but it's simply not offered at a time convenient for you to take it.

In spite of detailed planning, these things do happen. If they happen to you, you have to have a fall-back plan ready to go. Here are a few suggestions.

Investigate different time slots and alternate classes

If the needed class is offered early in the morning, around lunch time or late in the afternoon, your employer might cut you some slack and just not notice that you are running a little late coming in, taking slightly longer lunches or leaving work a bit early a few days a week. Don't try this unilaterally - get your immediate supervisor's permission to shorten up your work day. Offer to make up the time on another day, on the weekends, or during the non-class days. And make sure you do it.

You could also volunteer to take your vacation one hour at a time. I once managed to take a class doing exactly that. Again, your employer has to be cooperative.

You may be able to substitute another class for the one you can't get to during the day. This is especially true for electives. You may have had your heart set on Roman History to satisfy your Humanities elective, but since it's only offered at 2 PM, you can't take it. Look for something else to take in its place. Chinese Cooking at 7 PM may also satisfy that elective. Bite the bullet (or the egg roll), take the Cooking class and get on with your life.

The accelerated Intersession classes offered between the two long Fall/Winter and Spring Semesters at many schools are absolute killers - 3 or more hours a day, five days a week for two to three weeks or so. But at the end of that little crash course you have 3 more credits. Maybe the class you need is offered during an Intersession and you can use some vacation time to attend. Try to get a lot of sleep before you take an Intersession class, because you won't get much during this shortened, intense semester.

Also look at the short sessions most schools offer in the summer. These typically run five or six weeks, and, like Intersession classes, pack a lot of information into a very condensed time frame. Once again, you may have to sacrifice some vacation time or sick day accumulation to pull this off.

> **"I wasn't going to let one course get in the way. I looked around locally to find a course that would transfer."**
> *Valerie G. couldn't find an appropriate class in her primary school so she went somewhere else for it.*

Look at non-classroom credit opportunities

Go to the head of the department that is offering the class you need but can't attend and see if you can test out of it or do a project for it. The class might also be offered on television, available on videotape or DVD as a self-paced "correspondence" course, or be running on the Internet. Classes offered in these non-traditional formats may not actually appear in the class schedule that is published every semester. You may have to go hunt these down inside the department responsible for the class. And you will likely have to make some personal arrangements with the teacher handling the class.

Build your own class

You could try to round up a dozen or so other people who want to take the class at night, on a weekend or on the Internet and go to the administration with the list. Most administrations are always on the hunt for more ways to make money, and a filled-in-advance class is one of them. If they can find an instructor they might agree to offer the class to you and your recruits. Find out what the minimum class size is for that particular class. The department sponsoring the class will have this information. This tactic might be a long shot. Some classes may require so many warm bodies that it will be impossible for you to recruit enough people.

And, this needs to be an existing class, not a brand new one. Completely new classes have to go through an extensive review process that might take more than a year to get approved, prepped and staffed.

Go outside your school

There are probably other colleges in your area that are offering a class similar to the one you need at a time or in a manner that's more convenient to you. Round up the class schedules of those other schools, get some information on those classes, and take that research to your adviser. They may allow you to take the class at that other school and transfer it back in to your program. But be advised that you may have to go through the registration process at that second school, costing you unnecessary time, aggravation and money. If the second school has some sort of working arrangement with your college - and that is very common these days - you may be able to simply register for the class, take it and transfer it back into your school with minimum hassle. Your adviser should know if this is possible.

The last resort:
complain

If you can't get the results you need with the suggestions above, don't hesitate to complain loudly and regularly to the administration about being promised the availability of this class by someone in charge - your adviser. You kept all those signed schedules and notes taken during your counseling sessions, right?

If you make enough noise, they will probably find some way to accommodate you, if for no other reason than to shut you up. If you were promised that this class would be available at a time convenient to you and now it's not, you certainly have a legitimate complaint. Don't hesitate to voice it!

"In the past two years I only managed to get one class in at (my first college) because of my work schedule. And I took one at (another college) as independent study and had the credits transferred. In January I signed up for another class and there was a schedule change the day before I was to start. ....I had to drop out because I wouldn't have made it to all my classes."

Helen D. worked a rotating 3-shift schedule. The Dean at her original school was unable to help, but recommended she transfer to a four year non-traditional, non-residential college. She eventually earned her Bachelor's from there.

CHAPTER 19

Work Ahead

> "If I have a research paper due at the end of the semester, I'll often have it done 6 or 8 weeks after the course begins. Or as soon as I can, because I know myself. Otherwise I'll procrastinate right to the end."
> *Kevin R., 34, is married with two kids and worked a full time job. He started school at a community college and earned his Bachelor's degree in about ten years.*

Work ahead?! How can you possibly work ahead?

Aren't you already juggling the current demands of the courses you're in, plus your job, your family, some social life, etc? Under these conditions, is it possible to make time to get a head start on future course work?

It is. And if you can do it, you will find that in the long run it will actually <u>save</u> you time. Once again, the ability to do this is a reflection of your ability to manage time. Among adult college students, good time managers succeed, the not-so-good ones do less well, and the ones who can't manage time don't do well at all.

Here are a few hints.

Read the book before the class starts

If you plan carefully, you can buy the books for a given course several weeks ahead of time and read them before the class actually begins. Just blow through the books. Don't try to read every word in a text. Just scan it - read the first sentence or two of every paragraph, maybe just the first couple of pages of every chapter, or the headlines and subheads on every page. Look at the graphs and charts and illustrations. That old adage about a picture being worth a thousand words is true.

Review the Learning Objectives that are often found at the end of every chapter. They tell you what's important – and what's not.

This pre-reading technique has a couple of advantages. First, you'll be getting some advance warning of what to expect in the class. And second, reading something twice, with the reading periods separated by days or a few weeks, can increase your comprehension of that material quite a bit.

This is a good technique to use on those breaks between semesters. You've finished last semester's work, so you don't have to run at top speed. But you're still in study mode, so reading the texts for next semester at a fairly leisurely pace shouldn't even make you break a sweat. And by the time class starts, you'll be far ahead of everyone else in class. Your questions and comments in class will be much more intelligent – remember those extra Class Participation points in the Syllabus? And you should have much less trouble absorbing the material because you've already been through it once.

> **Kevin talks about the secret to good grades on research papers**
>
> "If I get homework assignments or research papers, I do them right away and then I try to contact the professor about those papers. Even if I've got to make up questions.
>
> ...I soon discovered that if I call the professor, talk to him a little bit about it, when it came time to grade the papers....he had already made a lot of the corrections for me, because I would hand it in early and say, would you look this over, I'm having some problems with this.
>
> ...In the end they have a hard time giving less than a good grade. Because they've already corrected it, they've already seen it and critiqued it."

Kevin R. with one of his many ploys to get through school with good grades. They must have worked: He graduated with a 3.95 GPA.

It also can't hurt to contact the teachers of your courses ahead of time to see if you can get the course outline and homework assignments in advance. In more and more schools this information is posted online and available year round.

You are just trying to develop a sense of what the course is all about. The course itself will give you the detailed knowledge. A few hours spent browsing the course material before you actually start the course will save you a lot of time later. It's a fact that material quickly scanned and then read thoroughly later stays with you better.

It's also a fact that teachers treat good students well. And trying to get a head start on a class puts you in that good student category, even before the class starts. And it increases your visibility in the class.

> **"I usually try to do most of my homework for the whole week on the weekends. Housework gets done whenever."**
> *Deanne L., married and the mother of two, originally started school in 1976. She finished her Bachelor's degree more than 20 years later.*

CHAPTER 20

Get To Know Your Teachers

> "There's no question I'd rather teach adults. Because they're upbeat, because they force me into extended preparation. They just are interested, which makes me feel so good about what I'm doing as an instructor."
> *Bill Sigismond, Director of the Office of Experiential and Adult Learning at Monroe Community College in Rochester, NY, also teaches in the Business Department there.*

Teachers are people too

Ask a hundred college teachers to define their favorite student and it's a pretty safe bet that about 95 of them will describe that student this way: older, employed, and probably attending part time. Many of these students may also be married or in some sort of relationship, and there are perhaps some children around, although there is no way for the instructor to know those details before they get to know each person in a given class.

That description sounds a lot like you, doesn't it?

Adult students, whether in night school, taking classes on weekends, using distance learning or some other delivery mode, are usually the favorite students with teachers simply because they are typically much better students.

And that's critically important to those people who stand in front of a classroom, because most people who teach don't do it for the money. Compared to what a similarly educated person could make in business, there just isn't very much money in it. (The average salary for teachers is well below the average wages of other white-collar occupations, according to the well respected American Federation of Teachers http://www.wsbtv.com/education/2326180/detail.html. The $44,367 average teacher salary in 2002 compares with $54,503 for mid-level accountants, $74,534 for computer system analysts, and $76,298 for engineers.)

These people teach because they love to help others learn. That's why they like adult students so much: adult students are just more interested in learning. And they're usually very enthusiastic about it in the process.

In general, the adult students actually care about being in school. Unlike the 18-year-olds, many of whom are still in their adolescent haze and still learning how to be responsible, adult students generally can be counted on to perform, and in most cases to perform quite well. They show up on time, don't talk in classes, understand the meaning of deadlines, and work very hard at their assignments. They don't come up with a lot of bogus excuses about why they missed a test or didn't hand in homework. They participate actively in class discussions, and because they have decades of experience in living, the ideas that they share with the rest of their classmates often bring the discussion into the real world, where the material being covered can be directly related to living. This makes classes more lively, more informative. And definitely more fun for all involved, including the teacher.

In short, adult students understand the meaning of personal responsibility, and they usually have no difficulty understanding that in the real world, people work together and share their lives in complex, meaningful ways. This is something that most 18-year-olds have yet to figure out. And the distinction is not lost on the teachers, who in general are working their tails off in the classroom and greatly appreciate a positive response to what they are trying to teach.

And because teaching is such a tough job, those same instructors very much like to teach adult students. Because they don't have to <u>teach</u> them. They merely have to help them learn. And there is a big, big difference.

> **"Not so much that they treated me any differently, but my attitude and...the attitude of the other non-traditional students was, we wanted to be there. We wanted to learn. And....we weren't the first ones out the door when class was up. ....So any difference in the way I was treated was because I gave the same respect to the instructor that I was being given."**
> *Kathleen C. started at her community college in 1971. She kept at it for nearly 30 years before she earned her Bachelor's degree.*

What kind of a person is your teacher?

Not all night school or weekend or distance learning classes are taught by full-time, tenured day school teachers. Many are taught by business people who work all day, just like you do. These adjuncts or part-time teachers have some special expertise in a given subject area, and teach a class or two every semester just because they like to teach. (It is a very rewarding experience.)

If you start school at your local community college - and the majority of adult college students do - what kind of a person can you expect to see at the front of your classroom? As noted in an earlier chapter, according to the 1993 National Study of Post-Secondary Faculty, sponsored by the Department of Education and conducted by the National Opinion Research Center at the University of Chicago, about 60% of the instructors have a Master's degree, 15% have Phd's, and 15% have Bachelor's degrees. About 55% of them are full time employees of the school. That means that 45% of them are part time teachers, and many of those will be business people teaching a class or two. Three quarters of them are married, and more than 55% of them have kids. Slightly more than half the average community college faculty are women, and the average faculty age is 47.

Notice anything about these characteristics? Aside from their education, these people bear a striking resemblance to someone you know very well: yourself! They can generally be described as married, working adults with children. They are, in most important ways, people just like you. They have much more in common with you than they do with the 18-year-olds.

And many of them will have backgrounds and experiences that will be very similar to yours. To many of these people, mention of November 22, 1963, Vietnam, the moon landing, Woodstock, miniskirts, Watergate, the Reagan Era, the Challenger accident, or Monica Lewinski will not be references to some obscure piece of history. It will remind them of something that they actually lived through!

Will sharing some common history with your instructor help you directly? Every teacher-student relationship is different, of course. But it certainly seems as if it couldn't hurt.

Which instructor type should you choose?

Usually you will have no choice about what type of instructor you have for a given class. If by some chance you do, there are pros and cons between the full-time teachers and the part-time, business types who teach in their area of expertise. The full-time teachers may be better prepared and have a better theoretical grasp of the material, only because they teach it all the time. The business people, on the other hand, are often more enthusiastic, can probably bring some real world, hands-on experience to the subject that full-time teachers may lack, and may be more willing to cut you a little slack now and again because they understand what it's like to work all day and go to school at night (if that's the way you're going). You might be surprised to learn how many part-time instructors earned their degree the same way you're earning yours: one course at a time, over years of going to school, as a working adult.

> "....make sure that you don't allow a chasm (to grow) between yourself and your instructors. I think it's extremely beneficial to know that they are not the enemy. That they really do want the best for you."
> *Patrick A., 46, married, working and the father of two small children, finished his Bachelor's degree with a 3.6 GPA.*

These people can help you

Most teachers who choose to teach adults can be very helpful to you. For starters, with classes that are predominantly adults, they often structure their course content to get rid of the miscellaneous, relatively unimportant fluff that is in every course...the BS. Trust me: it's in every course. These instructors know that you are much too busy for make-work assignments. They understand completely that what you really want out of a given course is the three or four credit hours. Knowledge would be nice, certainly, and they (and you, of course) will try very hard to transfer that knowledge. But they know that your bottom-line goal in sitting in that room or on the other end of that Internet connection for all those weeks is the credit hours, pure and simple.

These people tend to be no-nonsense in their approach to teaching and course content. You will have to work, and probably work fairly hard. As a general rule they demand a higher level of academic performance of adults. (You can thank all of the adult students who came before you for that, because they consistently outperform the younger students. And teachers now pretty much expect that.)

But most of the teachers of adults get rid of the BS and concentrate on the core material in a course. Their assignments tend to be straightforward, and they may often be willing to bend the rules a bit in terms of attendance, homework, deadlines, etc. for you because they understand that you have a long list of other responsibilities. You still have to do the work. And you still have to show up and take tests and write papers. But it is very likely that you will be held to a somewhat different standard of administrative (not academic) performance than an 18-year-old, particularly if you are making a genuine effort to succeed in the class.

No matter what teacher you wind up with, you can be reasonably certain that they like teaching older, more experienced students. Use this positive attitude. Try to introduce yourself to your instructor early in the semester. This shouldn't be too hard. The good teachers will make an effort to get to know their students' lives and expectations in some detail, because they know that adults lead very complicated lives that can sometimes interfere with their schooling.

It's not unheard of for teachers and adult students to continue the interaction after class in some sort of social setting - a cup of coffee, maybe a drink at a local restaurant. If you get an offer like this, you should probably take him or her up on it. Letting your teacher get to know you more fully as a person can only help. Especially if you need some sort of special break because of work or family obligations.

"With me, all of my teachers have understood. I've got a family, I've got a husband. And if something doesn't get done and I go to talk to them about it, they don't have a problem. They'll say, look, we'll make some other arrangements. ....With the younger kids, ...some of them don't even try to get their work done. And the teachers aren't going to help them."

Deanne L., 39, married, working and the mother of two children, went to college for more than 22 years to earn her Bachelor's degree.

CHAPTER 21

Dealing With The Bureaucracy

> "I've gotten two particularly senseless letters that say, you need to complete .... these courses. And what they are, are the courses I'm .... actively engaged in taking, but I haven't completed yet because I'm not done with them. And they say, you need to complete these. Well, of course I need to complete them. In 8 weeks I will have and you could have saved the paper and postage."
> *Patrick A. commenting on dealing with the bureaucracy at his college.*

Colleges are basically big businesses whose "product" is educated students

Like all bureaucracies, they have rules and regulations and systems and procedures to help them function more smoothly and efficiently. And while you may disagree about how much sense a given rule makes or how a certain system operates, you probably aren't going to be able to change it, at least not easily or in a short period of time, if at all.

Your college catalog or student handbook has all the rules and regulations in it. A lot of them are just plain old common sense, but you should probably scan the catalog anyway. You may find some really obscure rule that could cause you difficulty if someone decided to enforce it. It can't hurt to spend a few minutes going through the campus laws.

> **"We're making it easier to register, easier to get credit outside the classroom. (We're offering) a lot of workshops to build their self-confidence."**
> *Bill Sigismond, Director of the Office of Experiential and Adult Learning at Monroe Community College.*

Registration

Your first taste of the bureaucracy in your school will come when you try to register for classes. I say 'try' because there's a possibility that the first time you attempt to register you won't manage to do it. You will be short some required piece of paper, or you will not have completed some form correctly, or you will need to take some sort of test(s) or placement exam.

This book won't help you much with registration. Every school is different in terms of what they require you to have in the way of paper work and what they expect you to do.

In general you will probably want to have some proof of who you are and where you live - important so you don't get zapped with that usually higher out-of-area tuition. A drivers license will usually do the job, although they may require a birth certificate, a passport, a utility bill or some other proof.

You may also have to produce a high school diploma and transcript or a GED certificate and scores, although this would be unusual for a community college, especially if you were just registering for a single class. Many four-year colleges require passing scores in either the ACT or SAT tests, while most community colleges do not require this.

As an aside, community colleges are normally 'open enrollment.' This means that just about anyone can walk in, register, and take a course. Some small percent of applicants to community colleges won't qualify for entrance because of abnormally low placement exam scores or abysmally bad high school performance, and those students would be sent back to a GED-level system to bring their skills up to college-entrance level. That scenario likely does not apply to most adult students.

Although you won't be required to take an entrance exam like the SAT, you will probably be required to take a placement exam to check your math and writing skills. The four year school that you ultimately transfer into will likely waive a SAT test requirement too. By the time you get to that four-year school you have already demonstrated that you are capable of doing college-level work, which is what the SAT is designed to predict. In any event, don't let the four-year school bully you into taking an entrance exam if you are going there after finishing two years of your program at a community college. They may ultimately force you to take it, but you can probably make a pretty strong case for not taking it. And that can save you time, money and grief. Don't give up without a fight!

More and more colleges, aware of the importance of adult students on their bottom line, are setting up special registration systems for them. These are usually designed to segregate you from the kids and accommodate your different schedule.

Telephone registration is very common - all you need is a credit card number or a billing address. Registration over the Internet is evolving rapidly. Either of these is preferable to visiting the school personally, unless you need to talk with an adviser. And although you can take your first class without ever seeing an adviser, you shouldn't take any more than that or you may wind up taking courses that won't count toward your degree.

BIG NOTE: Registering by phone or internet is OK, but only if you are <u>absolutely certain</u> of what you have to take. And the only way to be certain is if your schedule has been carefully planned in advance in detail by an adviser.

> **"I had to take the Transitional Studies English and Math. And they helped. I wasn't like a waste of my time. It helped me. I had been out of school for so long."**
>
> *Joyce M. had to complete two non-credit preparatory classes to prepare her for college-level work. They must have helped: She finished college in the Honor Society and had a 3.8 GPA.*

Some schools require you to take assessment tests that measure your skill levels in certain basic areas such as reading, writing and math. Note that if you fall below a certain level in these tests you may be required to take non-credit remedial or preparatory courses to qualify for the basic, credit-bearing courses. And you will be charged for these remedial courses.

If your assessment test scores indicate that you need to take preparatory or remedial classes, just take them. Sure, they cost money, and they cost time. But they will also make your life much easier when you get to the real, credit-bearing courses, because you will have had a firm foundation in those courses by virtue of the remedial classes you just finished.

You will, of course, have to fill out a registration form and probably part with some amount of money. Get used to this: colleges are very inventive when it comes to getting money from you.

Note that if your company has a tuition reimbursement program, some schools may defer payment of the tuition with the understanding that they will be paid when the course is finished, perhaps directly by your company.

Many colleges require medical histories, and in some cases, the results of an actual physical examination by a doctor. You will almost certainly be asked to produce proof that you have been given immunization shots for some common diseases, including measles, mumps and rubella among others.

If you are a military veteran, have your DD-214 discharge papers handy. Ask for an appointment with the Veteran's Affairs counselor. Some of your military courses may get you credit or you may have some financial aid coming.

Although many schools - particularly community colleges - do not require personal interviews for admission, you should talk with a counselor or adviser at the admission stage to avoid taking a class that may ultimately do you no good toward your degree. These people can help you a lot, and in any event you should plan on talking to one ASAP.

Note: There is a difference between being registered and being matriculated. Anyone can register and attend courses in most colleges. It's mostly a matter of paper work and money...you fill out some of the first and give the school some of the second. Whizbang - you're registered.

A *matriculated* student is one who has applied for and been accepted into a specific degree program. Most colleges will not let you apply for financial aid, register for more than part-time study, or actually receive a degree unless you are matriculated. It pays to choose a program and matriculate as early as possible. And for this you are going to have to sit down with an adviser.

> **"I check (all) my records periodically. .... I try not to get a parking ticket because I don't want to pay for it. .... (And) I try to make sure my health record is up to date. It's very important, because you get asked to leave if it's not."**
>
> *Bette B., the mother of two, earned her Associate's and her Bachelor's while in her 40s.*

Parking regulations

Parking is viewed as a fund-raising opportunity at most colleges. And if you aren't careful at most schools, you will be helping your college make a lot of (your) money.

There is almost nothing you can do about the often-Byzantine parking rules on many campuses. Forget that they may not be fair, make any sense, are enforced capriciously and carry hefty fines if violated. Just make sure that you thoroughly understand what the rules are, and then follow them to the letter.

Sharing a parking pass with someone else can often save you a few bucks. Taking public transportation to school pretty much eliminates having to buy a parking pass. Most schools have parking meters that can be used for those occasional trips to the library. For that matter you may be able to use them all the time if you like, although they are usually pretty rare compared to the spaces allocated to those students with parking permits. And over time they will probably cost you more money than the parking permit.

Library hours and cards
You will probably be using the library quite a bit. Your student ID will likely get you full library privileges, but it is possible that your school might require a separate library card. A phone call to the library or a review of the student handbook will tell you.

Find out when your library is open and write the hours down on a little card. Tape it to the inside of your notebook. Note that hours might change from one semester to another; hours in the summer and around holidays in particular might be reduced. Write the library's direct dial phone number down as well. You might be able to save yourself a trip by calling ahead to find out if they are open or have a particular book. You may also be able to access their electronic card catalog from your computer using the internet, saving you a trip to find a book or journal they don't have. Write this internet address down or put it on your favorites list in your browser so you can get to it quickly.

If you don't remember exactly how libraries are organized from your days in high school all those years ago, don't worry. Most schools run some sort of library familiarization tour or class. Take it. It will be time very well spent. Beginning English and/or writing classes often include a get-acquainted session in the library too.

Most schools have completely discarded the old card catalog that you remember from years ago. At a minimum they no longer keep it up to date.

Instead most use a computerized indexing system that will likely be a little intimidating the first time you use it. If you have any computer skills at all that fear won't last. And the new computerized systems are much faster and generally easier to use than the card catalog.

> **"If you have any outstanding bills they will not release your grades. If you have a library book out, you won't get your grades."**
> *Karen D., 46 and the single mother of four, started school in the early 70s. Nearly 30 years later she had earned her Bachelor's degree and was working on her Master's.*

Labs and computer rooms

Some courses are taught in two parts: a classroom portion and a lab portion. These are often in two separate rooms and at different times. The classroom is just that. The lab will be filled with the hardware or other special purpose gear you need for the hands-on portion of the class.

Most hard science courses - Biology, Physics, Chemistry, Geology, Botany, Anatomy, Physiology, and the like, and most engineering and technical classes - have lab sections. Ditto for courses involving computers. These could include basic computer skills classes, writing courses, desktop publishing and graphic design classes, and classes devoted to specific pieces of computer software such as word processing, spreadsheets, page layout, photo manipulation, web site design etc.

The lab section of most classes is a separately scheduled component of the class; you will sign up for it when you register for the class itself. It will be held at a different time and in a different place from the classroom component of the class. Your course schedule will spell this out, and in many cases you will have some choice about the day and time of the lab, which gives you some needed scheduling flexibility.

Computer facilities on some campuses provide extended hours. But just like the library, you need to know what those hours are. When you find out, write them down, along with the direct dial phone number, and paste it to the inside of your notebook.

Note that on many campuses you will find computer-equipped classrooms hiding under a lot of different names. The Student Computer Center is of course one. But word processing classes, graphic and web design courses and similar classes will also be taught in special classrooms. The Computer Department will have its own collection of classrooms. The Writing Center will probably have some computers available. Libraries often have some. And if your school has an Accounting center, check there too.

So if you need to use a computer, don't get discouraged just because the Student Computer Center is full or closed. Wander around a little bit. Ask some questions. There are probably a lot of other computers available for use. You just have to find them.

If you have a computer and internet access at home, check to see if you can access the campus computer from your home if necessary. It can save you a trip to school.

And more and more campuses are equipped with hot spots, places that allow wireless access for laptops with wireless capability. If you are already at school, this can save you the time and trouble of finding a free computer if you have a laptop with wireless capability.

Most schools provide students automatic access to the Internet and the World Wide Web, either through the computers in the Library, the ones available in the campus computer center, or from the hotspots.

Check to see if you have this access. It can considerably shorten research time for many of your projects - if you know how to use it. If the school offers free classes on how to use the Internet and the World Wide Web, and you don't already know, take them. It'll be some of the most valuable information you'll ever get from the school.

Many schools will also issue you an email account. This will live on the school's servers, and will allow you to communicate with other students, the faculty and staff, various departments within the school, and, of course, the world at large. Although college computing facilities are usually pretty reliable, they are also usually very large (I'm told that my community college has more than 5000 computers on its network) and may occasionally experience technical problems that make them inaccessible for periods of time. If you want access to email 24/7, you might be better off to subscribe to a commercial service like AOL, Yahoo or MSN.

"I don't check my records. I'm terrible with any kind of forms. I just keep my fingers crossed. I recently got a letter saying that I have completed the right things. Some people got big surprises this year. They gotta go around begging for waivers and things."

Ann H. started school in the early 1990s at her local community college, got her Associate's degree, transferred to a four-year school as a Junior, and earned her BA about eight years later.

CHAPTER 22

Campus Resources

> "I'm one of those students who does use the library...A lot of students do their whole papers from the Internet, but I've always gone to the library and I still use it. And I use the Internet as well."
> *Karen D., 46 and the single mother of four, started school in 1972. It took her 26 years more to earn her Bachelor's Degree.*

Most colleges are small cities

Your college is much more than just a place to go learn. It provides a number of other functions, and includes a very wide variety of resources. Most of them are available just by showing your student ID card. While not all schools will have everything noted below, and non-traditional or distance learning programs may offer only a few or none of these possibilities, campus-based programs will usually include most of them. Your college catalog will describe what's available. Check the maps that are often posted in the campus hallways too.

You may want to spend a few hours some day just wandering around and checking some of these resources out. While many of them are specifically designed to support learning, a lot of them are there simply to provide convenience for students and faculty and staff alike. These can save you valuable time, increase your schedule flexibility by saving you from having to run somewhere to mail a letter, cash a check or grab a meal, and, in some cases, provide you with discounts on products and services.

Let's have a look around....

Library

All campus-based schools should have a library of some sort. Larger schools may have extensive library facilities, and it would not be unusual to see collections with hundreds of thousands of books, magazines, newspapers, tapes, videos, DVDs, CDs, records, microfilms, etc., along with an on-line catalog that may include the holdings of dozens of other area public and private libraries in addition to the one on your campus. Your library may also offer photocopying, computer terminals with access to the Internet and the World Wide Web, computers with software for writing papers, doing spreadsheets, etc., quiet study areas, and small meeting rooms that can be reserved. Most libraries participate in an inter-library loan program, which allows you to borrow books and other materials not in your campus collection from other libraries.

> **"I do a lot (of my research) over the Internet. And I have a program on my computer that allows me to access the library catalogs."**
> *Andrea W., 47 and the single mother of one, started school in 1967. Thirty-three years later she finished her Bachelor's degree.*

Learning centers
These are usually special purpose study facilities equipped and staffed to help you with work involving a specific subject: writing, math, accounting, the hard sciences like physics, biology, geology, chemistry, etc., the social sciences such as psychology, sociology and so forth, computer-related subjects such as graphic design and specific software programs. Many of these centers have on-site tutors, self-paced video tapes and/or computer programs to help you understand the material better. If you're having problems with a particular subject area, this is a good place to look for help.

Computer center/
Internet access/
Electronic learning center
Most schools of any size will have a campus computer center where you can go to write papers and do other types of assignments where a computer and software can help - accounting spreadsheets, graphic and web design projects, work with databases, math assignments, etc. Computers will commonly include both PC/Windows and Macintosh operating systems, and a library of software titles.

And more and more schools have 'hot spots' – locations where your wireless laptop can access the school's wireless network, so you're not dependent on the availability of school computers to do work.

In many schools these capabilities will be just the beginning. Your school's center may also include access to the World Wide Web and the Internet, and provide VCRs/DVDs and video and audio tape systems to use for information captured in those formats. These centers may also provide access to slide projectors, overhead projectors, and film projectors.

Counseling

Your school undoubtedly offers advising related to selecting courses and majors, and you should avail yourself of those offerings. But they may also offer other types as well, including personal counseling and financial counseling. These people are usually PhDs in Psychology, Counseling, Education or some related field, and are there to help people with personal, non-academic problems in a private, no-fee setting. Sometimes we just need somebody to talk to. Your counseling office may be the place to find a friendly ear.

**Job/employment/
career counseling**

One of the primary functions of higher education is to equip people with the skills they need to hold down a job. So virtually all schools provide some form of employment services for their students. It's not unusual to see a separate department staffed with employment counselors, computers connected to local, state and national job registries, bulletin boards full of job listings, and small libraries detailing requirements for specific careers. If you need to find work, or you're thinking about changing careers, this is probably a good place to start.

Most of these facilities will also provide help in generating cover letters and resumes, and may actually offer to videotape mock job interviews that can be later critiqued.

Many of these centers will also do psychological profile testing, to help you learn more about areas that you might have some real talent in.

Book store

Campus book stores don't just sell books anymore. Many of them resemble small department stores, with shelves full of clothing, office supplies, gift items, greeting cards, snack food, etc. One of their biggest attractions is their deals on computers and software. It's not unusual to find prices noticeably lower than your local retailers for computer hardware and software. If you need computer-related products, it's wise to check here first. Your student ID card could save you some money.

As an aside, most computer hardware and software makers offer deals on their products to students and faculty alike. The savings can often be quite significant. The company website is a good place to start your search. The Apple Computer website at http://www.apple.com/education/hed/students/discounts.html is a good example.

**Athletic/exercise/
health facilities**

Practically all campuses have some sort of athletic facility, and many of them are as good as anything in your community. And guess what? Most of the time you can use these facilities for free, simply because you are a student. Swimming pools, workout and weight rooms with all the latest machines, tracks, basketball, tennis and handball courts - all are usually available to students. Note that hours may be somewhat restricted since many of these are being used as classrooms for phys ed-related subjects.

> "My school library is just more equipped to handle what they're teaching than the public library. I know I can come here and get (what I need) at any time."
> *Evelyn S. went to school for nearly 25 years to earn her Bachelor's.*

Medical/health services

Most campuses will have a nurse's office, and large campuses may actually have a physician on staff, at least for part of the day. Although most of these are not set up to provide on-going care to anyone, they are usually equipped to deal with minor illnesses, bumps and bruises and emergencies. You should at least know where your school's medical office is and what hours it is open. If you can't find it, ask the campus security folks where it is.

Student center

This is a catch-all term often applied to a surprisingly wide variety of things collected in more or less one location. These may include recreational facilities like TV, pool tables, card tables and video games. Many newer facilities include "hot spots" – wireless internet access points for people with laptop computers and wireless PDAs. You may see conference rooms, study areas, public telephones, or bulletin boards to provide information on apartment and housing rentals, car rentals, airline travel and vacations. There will often be some sort of lounge area, and it may include some of the facilities noted below.

Vending machines

Wherever you find students, you will find vending machines - soft drinks, coffee, potato chips and pretzels, cookies, candy and other snack foods, perhaps even stamps and office supplies like pens and pencils. These can be widely scattered on some campuses, but you will often find a collection of them near the student center.

Bank/check cashing/ stamps/tickets

A little short on cash? Need to mail some bills? Like to see a movie this weekend or go to the game? Many campuses have a window or an office that provides these convenient services and many more. You can cash a check, buy stamps, bus passes, money orders, tickets to movies, plays, sporting events etc. And in some cases - movies are a good example - tickets cost less here than they would if you went to the theater box office. ATMs are common in these areas.

Food service

Most schools will offer some sort of cafeteria, although in some cases it may be nothing more than a collection of vending machines and some tables. A lot of schools, particularly those which have a food service or restaurant/hotel/hospitality industry major, may offer much, much more, up to and including something resembling fine dining. Bear in mind that many of these are learning experiences for students, so the level of overall quality may not be what you're used to, either in food or service. But the prices are usually right.

> "What we do is a lot of brokering - sending people where they will find support services. Traditional colleges provide a world that is self-contained unto itself. The counseling center is here, the career services office is there, the library is there. ....One of the definitions of Empire State College, one of the distinguishing hallmarks, is that we use the community as our campus."
> *Sharon Grigsby recruits adult students for Empire State College, the non-traditional college of the State University of New York system.*

Child care

This is a major consideration for a lot of students, and many schools have responded by creating on-campus day care facilities. Be warned that there may be a waiting list. Schools sometimes do not publicize the availability of this service because they don't want to be overwhelmed with requests that they can't fill. You may have to go looking for this. And, of course, you will have to pay for this service.

Services for students with disabilities

Virtually all colleges provides a wide range of services for disabled students. These usually include special advising and registration procedures, help in getting financial aid, sign language interpreting, note taking, tutoring, special testing considerations, TDD and computer access, help with access to the campus and its facilities and other services. There will probably be a special office on campus or someone in the Counseling or Registration office designated to help these students.

Veteran's office

Many colleges have special services available for vets. These may include help with counseling, financial aid, and assistance with forms and documentation required by the VA or other organizations. Check with the Advising/Counseling Center or Registration office to locate these services.

> "We have an in-house program that shows adults how to develop a portfolio (for Credit By Evaluation) and then get credit for that portfolio."
> *Bill Sigismond runs the Office of Experiential and Adult Learning at Monroe Community College in Rochester, NY.*

Adult student workshops

Schools that are used to dealing with adult students will often have special workshops set up to help these students make an easy, productive transition back into the learning environment. Workshops may include study skills, note taking tips, time management, test anxiety, stress management, self-esteem, and career guidance and evaluation. These short courses are usually free and quite helpful.

Campus media

Many campuses have their own radio stations, and some even have their own TV stations. These broadcasts may or may not be available off the campus, and their choice of programming may not be to your taste. But if you've always wondered how broadcast stations operate - or had an urge to be on the air! - go check them out. Did we mention newspapers? Most schools have at least a campus newspaper, and many have campus literary or poetry magazines as well. These are great opportunities to get real-world experience in these specialized areas. And there may even be some credit opportunities with some of these!

Entertainment

You might be very surprised at the amount of inexpensive - or actually free - entertainment available on your campus. It will probably include plays put on by students from the Theatre/Drama or Communications departments, reasonably new or classic movies, art exhibits, dance recitals, musical groups, speakers and lectures, etc. Just check the bulletin boards in the halls.

Bulletin boards
And speaking of bulletin boards, you will probably find a lot of them sprinkled around the campus. The notices on them often make for interesting reading, and will usually include offers of ride sharing, books, apartments, roommates, things for sale, events and so forth.

Lost and found
This is probably located near or in the campus security service.

**Campus safety/
escort services**
This is the campus police department. If you have a security concern or want to complain about a parking ticket, this is the place to come. They will also normally provide escort services for people concerned about walking alone to their cars, etc.

Repair services
Schools with technical curriculums like automotive repair, appliance repair, electronic technician training and the like may be on the lookout for things that are broken so the students get real-world experience in fixing them. These services are often very inexpensive, or sometimes even free. The downside is that you may have to leave the item with them for a long time.

Medical/Dental/Optical Care/Massage Therapy
Schools that have programs in the medical/dental, optometric or massage therapy areas may offer free or reduced-price care as an incentive for their students to have people to practice on. This care is always carefully supervised by licensed professionals, and represents a good opportunity to get high quality care for less than market rates.

Clubs

A typical campus will have an amazing number of special interest groups or clubs: Honor Society, amateur radio, dance, stamp collecting, debating, political science, poker, chess, travel, foreign languages and many more may be organized. There may often be a variety of informal sports teams available to join as well. Watch the bulletin boards. Or check in at the Student Center, which is where many of them will have offices.

Campus tours

Want to locate all of these resources and some that are not even on this list? Your Registration office probably runs regular guided tours of the campus. It might be a fun way to spend a couple of hours.

> **"We have a Peer Mentoring program. These are people who are adult students and they meet individually with new adult students. We also have an Adult Hotline - anyone can call and we'll get back to them within 24 hours."**
>
> *Betty Smith counsels returning adult students at Monroe Community College in Rochester, NY. She was a returning adult student herself, and didn't start college until she was well into her late 40s. She ultimately earned a Master's Degree.*

CHAPTER 23

Grades, Grading And Grade Point Averages

> "I took a remedial math class. I am so glad I did, because I have math anxiety. Terrible. And I don't think I would have made it without that. So it was a good step for me."
> *Bette B. has a perfect 4.0 Grade Point Average.*

Grading can be a confusing proposition sometimes

This chapter will try to simplify it a bit. Most colleges use a letter grade system: A, B, C, D, E, F and I(ncomplete) and (W)ithdraw. An A is usually described as Excellent, a B is above average, C is average, D is usually the minimum passing grade, and E or F are failing. Many schools do not use the E grade, preferring instead to use F(ailing).

Some schools use the + and - system in combination with the letter grades described above. If your school uses +/-, then your grade system looks something like this: A, A-, B+, B, B-, C+, C, C-, D+, D, D- and F. The minimum passing grade under this system might be as low as a D-. Note that there is no A+ grade at many schools. The feeling is that since A is perfect and you can't get any better than perfect, A+ doesn't exist.

These letter grades are the result of numerical grades given on tests, papers, homework assignments, quizzes, etc. If your instructor uses a system that converts numbers to letter grades, it can have a significant effect on your final letter grade. Here are a few hints on how to keep that letter grade up where you want it, which is to say, as high as possible.

Check your syllabus or course information sheet

Your professor should go over his or her grading scheme during the first class, and will normally have it written down on the class syllabus or course information sheet, which is just a description of what the class will cover and when it will cover those particular topics. Tests, quizzes and due dates for papers and projects should also be on this schedule. The syllabus will likely also include some administrative details like the policies for attendance, absences, lateness, sickness, class meeting schedules, off-campus field trips, etc.

If you don't get this information on grading at the first class, <u>ask for it</u> immediately after class. This information is very important, as it shows you, in black and white, how your grade will be determined. You need to know what it takes to get an A, a B, etc.

> **"You know, it's not like I'm an over-achiever. It's just that I enjoy my classes and I'm having fun with them. I love them. They're great classes."**
> *Deanne L. took 20 years to get her Bachelor's degree.*

Some typical grading schemes
A typical grading scheme might look like this:

100 points available:	
Paper 1:	15 points
Paper 2:	15 points
Class Quizzes (3):	30 points
Attendance (15 classes):	15 points
Class Participation:	15 points
Final Exam:	<u>10 points</u>
	100 points

Another one might look like this:

100 points available:	
Exam 1:	15 points
Exam 2:	35 points
Final Exam:	<u>50 points</u>
	100 points

Which one of these is the one you'd like to see on your syllabus? Phrased another way, which of these grading schemes is likely to give you the most trouble, and which is likely to help you the most?

System #1 is by far the most lenient. It gives you half a dozen different ways to earn points, and each is pretty balanced when compared to the others. None counts for more than 15 points. That means you could completely bomb two of these 15 point assignments and still pass the course. Or you could also miserably fail all the in-class quizzes and still pass.

Even blowing the final exam would only cost you a mere 10 points. If you had a good grade going into the final, failing it might not even affect your final letter grade. If you were really strong going into the final exam, you might actually be able to skip it entirely without effect on your final grade!

Note also that System #1 gives you credit just for showing up! If you make every class, you automatically get 15 points. If you participate in class - ask questions, try to keep the conversation going, add different viewpoints or examples to what the teacher is talking about - you could earn another 15 points. In a grading system structured like this, you can pick up about one third of the points you need for a decent grade just by coming to class and staying visible (and audible) to your teacher!

Let's look at system #2. This class would be very dicey unless you were just a super test taker. And not everyone is. Many people, in fact, are nervous about taking tests. Given a choice, they would prefer to write papers or participate in class or take a little, low-point quiz every now and then. This teacher, however, is not offering any of those possibilities.

This would be a bear of a class. If you blew the first exam, you would have to be nearly perfect on the next two to get a pretty decent grade. If you dumped the second exam, you could ace both the first and third exams and still fail this course!

Most teachers are more fair than the one shown in System #2. They know that different people learn in different ways, and they are aware that adults prefer more active involvement in their learning. And so they offer different alternatives to get points. In general, the more ways there are to get points in a class, the better off you will be.

Some teachers offer <u>extra points</u>. A class structured like this might have this sort of a grading system:

---

100 points available:

Paper 1:	15 points
Paper 2:	15 points
Class Quizzes (3):	30 points
Attendance (15 classes):	15 points
Class Participation: 15 points	
Final Exam:	<u>10 points</u>
	100 points

Bonus Point Assignments:
5 page research paper:	15 points
5 page book report:	15 points

This grading system is a gift - that's the only way to describe it! A perfect score in this class would be 100 points...but this teacher is giving you the opportunity to earn <u>130</u> points. If you are better with papers and writing assignments in general than you are with tests, go for the extra point assignments. You could do very badly on all three quizzes, blow off the final completely - and still do alright in this class. This teacher is clearly trying to help her students out, and she is very aware that different people have different styles of learning.

Some teachers structure their class around the standard 100 point total. From everyone's point of view that system is easy to understand and deal with. Depending on how many different components make up that 100 points, your class will be more or less fair.

A typical grading system might look something like this:

A = 96 - 100
A- = 91 - 95
B+ = 86 - 90
B = 81 - 85
B- = 76 - 80
C+ = 71 - 75
C = 66 - 70
C- = 61 - 65
D+ = 56 - 60
D = 51 - 55
F = 50 and below

You should have a chart or table that looks like this on your syllabus or course information sheet.

Some instructors use a grading system based on more than 100 points. Systems with 200 points are fairly common, and 300, 400, 500, even 1000 are not unheard of.

Why do instructors do this? Simply to give themselves some additional refinement in the grading process. Ten point quizzes become 20 points in a 200 point system, so the teacher can award you an 85% score, or 17 points, something impossible in a 10 point system. Here she would have to give you either 8 points or 9 points. And if you weren't quite good enough to get the 9, she would have to give you 8, even though she felt that you did better than 8. In most cases, systems which use more than 100 points are better for you.

> "I like to get notes back from my professors on the work that say, I hadn't thought of that, what an interesting way to present (that idea.)"
> Patrick A., 46, finished his Bachelor's degree in five years while still working nearly full time as a waiter. He continued on for his Master's Degree.

Grading on a curve

You will still run into teachers who grade on a curve, although this technique seems to becoming less popular. This system takes the highest grade in the class and makes it equal to 100, or a perfect score. Everyone else in class is judged against that highest score - the best performer in the class - rather than 100. A typical "curve" might look like this:

88.0 Highest grade in class	= 100
83.6	= 95
79.2	= 90
74.8	= 85
70.4	= 80
66.0	= 75
61.6	= 70
57.2	= 65

You can see what's going on here. If the top grade earner in your class actually got 100, and there was no curve, you would need to get 90 points to get a 90% grade. In this case, however, the best grade in the class is only an 88. Once your teacher decides that that 88 is equal to 100, your grade effectively goes up. And now to get 90 points - and the letter grade that goes with it - all you really need to earn is 79.2.

Teachers don't usually grade on a curve unless the class as a whole has done worse than expected, and the highest total grade in the room is noticeably less than perfect. This often happens when the teacher has changed something about the class and is using that "new" thing, whatever it is, for the first time. It could be a new text, a new set of quizzes, new tests, new assignments, new teaching technologies such as computers, the Internet, etc. If the class as a whole scores less than he would expect if they had been using the previous materials, he may compensate you for being guinea pigs by using a curve.

If you think that the class as a whole has done worse than the teacher expected, always ask that the class be graded on a curve!

You may not get it, but it does flag the instructor that you are aware that your class has not performed to historical levels. That may be enough to get the curve instituted. And that will be good news for your grade.

The no-point/
all letter grade system

You may also run into a teacher who does not use a point system at all. All of her assignments, tests, papers and so forth would be graded with a letter grade, rather than a number of points which are subsequently turned into a letter grade.

This is an important difference. An instructor who uses letter grades only must have some way to average those letters. In a point system this is easy. Just take the numerical grades, add them up and divide by the number of different grades: 60, 80 and 90 points = 230/3 = 76.67. And this 76.67 is equal to some letter grade that's already pre-determined. Simple.

But it's not that easy to average letter-only grades. What is the average of A, A-, B, B+ and D? Is this a B? A B+? A C+?

I don't actually know what grade would be assigned to a student with that particular collection of letter grades. But if your instructor is using only letter grades to determine your performance, you need to be aware of that right up front. A letter-only system would seem much more subject to the teacher's analysis and seemingly much more arbitrary than numerical grades. And while it <u>might</u> be a better deal for you, my hunch is that you will usually be better off with a numerically-based system that is ultimately converted into a letter grade.

> **"The second semester went much easier because I went from Bs to almost straight As. It was a big jump."**
> *Evelyn S., 41 and the married mother of two, took nearly 15 years to earn her Bachelor's degree. She finished with a 3.5 GPA and plans for a Master's degree.*

Grade Point Averages

Grade point averages are important in a variety of ways. Your GPA in a given course is the translation from the letter grade that you actually earn on a grade card to a number of points. This is a typical system:

```
A  = 4.00
A- = 3.67
B+ = 3.33
B  = 3.00
B- = 2.67
C+ = 2.33
C  = 2.00
C- = 1.67
D+ = 1.33
D  = 1.00
D- = 0.67
F  = 0.00
```

Grade point averages are based a system called quality points. Most of these schemes are based on a 4.0 system. If you earn an A in a three credit class, you would earn 4.00 quality points per credit x 3 credits = 12 quality points. If you had a B in another 3 credit class, you would have 3.00 quality points x 3 credits = 9 quality points.

Your GPA for that semester would then be:

4.00 x 3 = 12 points
3.00 x 3 = <u>9 points</u>
          21 points/6 hours attempted = 3.5 GPA.

A 3.5 GPA, by the way, would probably be high enough to get you on the Dean's List or Honor Roll in most schools. If you kept a 3.5 GPA all the way through, you would quite likely graduate with honors. And it would probably say that right on your diploma.

Why is the GPA important? For several reasons. As noted above, a GPA that is high enough - say 3.5 or above - will probably get you on the Honor Roll, the Dean's List, or in line to graduate with honors. You'd feel pretty good about that, and it would demonstrate once again what people who work with adult students already know: that they blow the doors off most younger students in grades.

A high GPA also looks pretty impressive on your transcript. If you're going to transfer to some other school, either from a community college into a four-year school to finish your Bachelor's or you are going on to grad school, a strong GPA will carry a lot of weight in acceptance criteria. And it may help you qualify for scholarship money.

You should recalculate your GPA every semester to make sure that what's on your grade report is accurate. To do that you need to save every grade card you get.

Your Records and Registration office can also confirm your GPA, and you may be able to access the information electronically through your school's web page. But just to be on the safe side, you should be able to calculate it independently. And that means you have to save your grade cards.

Your college's catalog will likely have a page or two devoted to GPA: what it is, how to calculate it, etc. Many schools have a GPA Calculator on their web sites that allow you to 'tinker' with your GPA, to see what better (or worse!) grades in forthcoming classes will do to your Grade Point Average.

Here's one: http://image-ination.com/test_maker/gpa.html

Narrative grading

Some colleges - SUNY Empire State College in New York State is one of them - have dispensed completely with numeric or letter grades. Their system is based on an end-of-course description/evaluation from the teacher of what the student accomplished during the course and how she accomplished it. These are usually only a page or two, but I have seen some that run four or more pages. They can be very detailed.

For those of us who went to grammar and high school when number or letter grades were the only kind handed out, this narrative grading scheme can be a bit confusing. Many of us are used to having a grade goal that is expressed as an "A", or "I want a 90%," or something like that. How do we respond when we are given several hundred words to describe our performance?

If your college is using narrative grading, somewhere in your catalog or course materials it will tell you that. Although the first time it happened to me it was a complete surprise. I missed the explanation in the catalog.

Narrative grading has the benefit of giving you a lot of detail about exactly how well you performed in a class, and most professors will specifically point out your strengths and weaknesses. In terms of information, the narrative grade is much superior to a letter or a number.

However, this grading scheme makes it impossible for you to keep track of a GPA, so at best you will have only a qualitative idea of how well you are doing. And if you want to transfer to another school, either to finish your Bachelor's degree or to go on for a Master's, the new school may give you a hard time about narrative grades, especially if their system is based on GPAs.

Many schools using narrative grading will also give you a letter or number grade if you ask for it. If knowing your GPA is important to you - or you think it will be important to a school you'll be transferring into - ask for it.

> **"They have to understand that when they come home, maybe their day is over with, but you're a student. Your day isn't over with. It will extend into the night hours sometimes."**
> *Dave P., 49, battled and beat cancer and earned his Bachelor's degree. His goal is a PhD.*

CHAPTER 24

Recheck Your Records Every Semester

> "I figured that if there was something wrong (with my records) they'd tell me."
> Deanne L. wondering just how accurate her school's records really are.

Colleges are big, exciting places
They are also businesses

And even though most young college students don't look at them like that, you certainly should. And as businesses, they tend to generate a lot of paper and keep a lot of records. And occasionally, someone, somewhere, will make a mistake in those records.

People get tired or aren't paying close attention to what they are doing. A simple keystroke error and Shazamm! Your A in English just turned into a D and dropped your grade point average, destroying your chances for a scholarship at the school you will be transferring into three years from now.

Your school's main computer has a programming problem, an Internet virus sneaks in through a security breach in the school's firewall, a power failure roars through the neighborhood, or the main office building gets hit by lightning. Zapp! You just disappeared from the rolls of Psych 101 and - five years from now - will be asked to take it.

Again.

The roof leaks and destroys a bunch of records. DripDrip!! Your entire fall semester just got tossed out.

Can't happen? It does happen, more often than you would think. A friend of mine discovered, when he went to apply to grad school, that his undergrad school had no record of him ever attending there. Ever! There had been a small fire in the records office some years earlier and several hundred student records had been completely destroyed. He vanished without a trace. It took him many months and the threat of legal action to get it rectified, and delayed him an entire year in his entry into graduate school.

Since your entire degree program depends completely on having passing grades recorded for x-number of courses of certain kinds, it is absolutely imperative that the records of your performance at your school be complete, current and accurate.

Your last semester before graduation is not the time to discover that someone forgot to enter that grade change you got three years ago that managed to bump you into passing a course that you were failing and would have to repeat. And that is not the time to find out that the teacher who got sick that last week of that English course years ago never passed her records on to her hastily-summoned replacement who filled in for three days - and you and twenty other people never got official credit for that class, and are still listed as (I)ncomplete.

Mistakes like this happen all the time in businesses all over the world - think they don't happen in campuses where a considerable amount of routine work is performed by 18-year-old work-study students? A glitch in your academic record can cost you a great deal of time, money and aggravation.

Note that in many schools a certain grade point average is required to graduate. It's a 2.0 (a C average) in my community college, and that's pretty typical. Also be aware that a certain GPA is required for admission to any college if you are transferring in. This GPA is typically 2.5 to 3.5, depending on the school and program you are going into.

But it's not just academic records that can get screwed up

Your college is also maintaining a lot of auxiliary information about you that has nothing to do with your academic performance. What kind? Here's a few scenarios.

Most schools will not graduate students who have unpaid parking tickets - and it's very easy to get tickets on most campuses. Ditto for library book fines or books that show up as never returned. The same is true for athletic equipment, computer equipment, etc. that was checked out. Add in cap and gown rentals, student association and lab fees, and so forth. And how are your medical records? Are all your shots up to date? Do they know that in the Records office?

The point here is that people can and do make mistakes in entering and maintaining information and natural disasters can and do happen once in awhile. To prevent these mistakes from affecting you, <u>you</u> <u>must</u> <u>keep</u> a duplicate, parallel set of records of everything you do while in school.

> **"I check all my records every semester. I make sure that they don't miss anything."**
> *Linda W., 41, originally started at her community college in 1979. About two decades later she finished her BA and went on for a Master's.*

What kind of records should you keep?
Here's a partial list:

- Grade cards from the end of semesters
- Canceled checks used to pay for classes, lab and student fees, books, parking tickets, etc.
- Receipts from those payments
- Any papers returned by teachers with grades and comments on them
- Written information from advisers, including suggested course schedules
- Medical records, particularly immunization records and excuses
    - written by a doctor for classes you may have missed for medical reasons.

Is this a pain in the butt? Yes. Is it absolutely necessary? Only if you want to be absolutely certain that <u>somebody</u> has records of your school performance that are complete and accurate. If you trust your school to do this for you, fine. But a lot of adult students don't.

Every semester you should go to the Records office and ask to see your academic record and any other important information that they are keeping on you, particularly as it relates to things that might affect your ability to either graduate or have your credits transferred to another school. As noted above, things like parking tickets and non-returned books and equipment can kick you out of the graduation line in a hurry.

You don't want a printed transcript, even though that's what they will probably tell you you need. A transcript that they will happily charge you a few bucks for, of course. You just want to quickly glance at your records for a few moments to spot any glaring errors that might have crept in over the last semester.

**You have a <u>legal right</u>
to inspect your records**

This right is guaranteed to you by the U. S. Family Rights and Privacy Act of 1974 (http://www.ed.gov/offices/OII/fpco/ferpa) and allows you to challenge any inaccuracies you find in those records. You also have the legal right to file complaints with the U. S. Department of Education about any failure of your school to allow you to inspect your records. The address to write to is in the Reference section and on the web site noted above.

If the Records office won't cooperate with you on this request, even after you've reminded them that they have a legal responsibility to do so, ask your adviser to bring your records up on his or her computer so you can get a look at them. A friendly teacher will probably have the same capability.

Note that these teacher-accessible records might only include academic records. People outside the Records office may not be able to access information about parking tickets, overdue library books, inaccurate medical records and so forth. So you really should try to gain access to your complete school records. And the Records office may be the only place where you can do that.

Don't be surprised! Check your records every semester!

> **"I keep a separate set of records. I keep track of everything myself."**
> *Lorene K., 41 and a single mother, worked full time as a waitress and went to school full time.*

CHAPTER 25

The Importance Of Having A Private Place To Study

> "Because my kids know that when my door is closed, it means mama is serious about her studying."
> Joyce M., 36 and a single mother of three, earned her Associate's degree in the late 1990s with a 3.8 GPA and has plans for a Master's degree.

A good place to study is essential

College is an almost constant struggle, especially for someone who works and is juggling a lot of other adult responsibilities like being in a relationship, raising a family, trying to maintain a house, etc., etc. Don't make it any harder by complicating the studying process.

Most people can't do reading or homework or write papers and reports in front of the TV set or on the dining room table. Many teenagers may think they can - but check their grades. The ones who are doing their studying in front of the one-eyed monster are probably failing.

Take this test: just sit in your kitchen or dining room or living room and pay attention to what's going on around you.

People are walking (or if you have little kids, running) in and out of the room, they are talking (or hollering if they're children), the radio, stereo or TV set is probably on, the phone is ringing, the dog wants to go out, people are raiding the refrigerator or wondering out loud about dinner, etc., etc.

These portions of your home are the public spaces, the places everyone feels free to travel to and through and make noise in. And they do. And they should be able to do those things in the areas that everyone shares. That's part of being a family.

That said, it does appear that some people actually <u>can</u> study in front of the TV or in a room that is constantly full of extraneous activity. These people just don't seem to be comfortable unless there is at least some level of background sound around them - the TV is going, the stereo is on, etc. If you are one of these rare individuals, you already know it, and will probably continue to do important, thinking-intensive tasks in front of the TV no matter what any book recommends. If this technique works for you, go for it.

> **"I've learned to shut the noises out. It took me a long time. It used to be, OK - everyone has to be absolutely silent, the TV has to be off, nobody move. Now, that's just not realistic! You can't expect everyone to sit there like that for hours every day."**
>
> *Ann H., shares her family room study space with a husband, a young grammar school child and the family dog. She managed to graduate with a 3.75 GPA.*

Studying is the most importante activity in college

But no matter where or how you do it, studying is probably the single most important aspect of going to college. The time you spend reading your texts, doing research or working on papers or other assignments is what really counts. These are the tasks that earn the grade. And that grade is what earns the credits. Get enough of those credits and you have that piece of paper. And that's really what all of this effort is for: that coveted college degree. So the connection between studying and graduating is pretty clear.

Unless you are one of those unusual individuals who can study in the midst of chaos, you definitely need a private space to study, preferably one with a door on it. This study area doesn't have to be terribly big, just large enough to accommodate a small desk, a chair, some decent lighting and a handful of standard reference books. If you have a computer system - and you probably should - that should be in there too.

During those times when you are studying, that space must be private - not shared with anyone else in the family. Make sure your spouse and kids understand that when the door is closed they cannot interrupt except for life-threatening emergencies. And then enforce that rule. For most of us, effective studying requires privacy and relative quiet.

> "I tried going to the library. But it's hard not to be around the papers that you need. You can't cart everything around with you."
> *Andrea W., 47 and the single mother of one child, used a spare bedroom in her home for studying.*

Finding and furnishing your study space

If you have a spare room in the house that's just filled with miscellaneous junk, clean it out, have a garage sale, take your partner or the whole family to dinner with the proceeds and then turn that space into your studying area. Put your mark on it just as you would an office at your work - pictures, plants, sayings on the walls, etc, etc. Make it yours.

But your studying space doesn't need to be as large as a spare room. I once built a tiny little office under a stairway in the basement of the apartment we were renting. The "desk" was just a piece of 3/4" plywood jutting out from the back of the stairs and supported on old dining room table legs that I found in the trash. I had a plain wooden chair in front of it, and I put lighting in there using an extension cord and a clip-on light. A couple of other pieces of plywood served as bookshelves over my head. This little room didn't have a door, just a curtain on a rod, but since it was in the basement there was no traffic around it. It was smaller than most closets. But it was private and quiet, and those were its most important characteristics. It did the job.

If you have no spare room in your house, your basement or attic may be a possibility. Ditto for the garage if it can be maintained at a comfortable temperature. Perhaps there's a corner of your bedroom that can be used. Several of the students interviewed for this book did a lot of their reading and note taking in their cars. A number studied at work, before work began, on their lunch hours, or after work. One used the family camper parked in the driveway. The public or school libraries are also possibilities. It doesn't really matter where you find the space. It just has to be quiet enough for you to study in, relatively private and accessible when you need it. A permanent space at home is obviously the preferred solution, but other locations are also possibilities.

> **"I try to study more in school. Believe it or not, some of my best studying is done in my car, with a cup of coffee and a pack of cigarettes."**
> *Lorene K., 41, earned an Associate's degree while working a full time job and attending school full time. She went on for her Bachelor's.*

Keep everything you need for studying in that room: computer system with Internet access, pencils and pens and highlighters and paper and pencil sharpener, dictionary, thesaurus, writing and style manuals, encyclopedia if you have one. You don't need any excuses to get up and leave the room to find a pen or the dictionary, etc. Don't give yourself any reason to interrupt the studying process.

Put the class progress grid we talked about earlier right up over your desk, where you'll see it every time you look up. It'll remind you of what you are doing all this for.

Pay careful attention to your lighting. Make sure you have plenty of it right over your desk, and that at least some of it can be adjusted a bit to compensate for changes in outside lighting or the present condition of your eyes, which are probably more sensitive to light after a long day of working and going to class.

And admit to yourself that the older you get, the more sensitive your eyes become to lighting changes. Older eyes see less well in low light conditions. You've probably noticed this effect while driving at dusk. And as we age our eyesight becomes less acute. By the time we reach 40 or so, many of us - this author included - discover that we need bifocals. If you suspect your eyesight is not what it used to be, get yourself in to your neighborhood optometrist for a check up.

College is very reading and writing intensive, and you need to keep your eyes in their best condition possible. Vision problems can normally be corrected, and that will be one less thing you'll need to struggle with. Doing the work will be challenge enough: don't spend time and energy fighting the condition of your vision too.

Fluorescent lighting is generally not as good for working as incandescent lighting, which is softer, not as harsh and can usually be directed to where you need it. If you have a choice, avoid fluorescent lights in your study area. Go with small desk or floor lamps which can be adjusted to form a "puddle" of light on your desk or over your reading chair.

You will be doing a very large amount of reading, so where you do that is important. Whether you do it at your desk, in a recliner, a straight back kitchen chair or sprawled on your floor is completely up to you. You should be comfortable when you read. But not so comfortable that you are nodding off. Experiment a little with different locations.

Check and adjust the ergonomics of your desk and chair. Desks are normally about 30" off the floor, but yours might need to be a bit higher or lower, depending on how you're put together. Adjustable height office chairs are recommended, as they allow you to change your position relative to your desk surface. Most of them have adjustable backs as well.

The surface area of your desk should be large enough to accommodate at least several open books at once, probably more. Research papers in particular usually require the use of a number of books or magazines or articles or downloads from the Internet, and it's not at all unusual to have to jump back and forth from one source to another when writing. Every piece of paper you're using should be readily accessible if possible - it will save you time and make the work easier.

Pay some attention to the way the desk, chair and lighting all work together. You are going to be spending hundreds, probably thousands of hours working here - make sure it is as close to perfect as you can get it. But understand that you will be fine tuning this space for months if not longer. The important, immediate concern is to capture some space in your home and equip it as well and as completely as you can.

As an aside, if you need a desk, chair, filing cabinet or some other office item, check the business auctions listed in your newspapers. There are usually some tremendous bargains available in used office furniture.

"They know that if the door is closed, they really need to be bleeding from three places before they come in. But if they really need a hug or something, they'll come in."

Valerie G., 38, moved her two grammar school age daughters into one bedroom and used the now-vacant bedroom as her office. It took her more than 20 years to earn her Bachelor's Degree.

CHAPTER 26

Studying And Note-Taking

> "There's lots of stuff at home that requires my attention. So frequently I'll have dinner....then start my work at 10:30 at night. I'll get to bed at 2 or 2:30 AM."
>
> *Patrick A. had a four and an eight year old and worked 20+ hours a week in addition to going to college full time. He earned a BA and went on for his Master's.*

Buffing up your study skills can save you time and energy

As noted in the previous chapter, studying is probably the most important aspect of going to college. It is what drives grades, which drive credit, which drive your graduation. If you are returning to school after ten, twenty, thirty years of being away from formal education, you are probably not used to methodically absorbing and categorizing knowledge. Don't let this discourage you! You actually have these skills, and you use them on an informal basis all the time as an adult. Your entire adult life has been spent learning one thing or another - how to drive a car, how to do your job, how to manage money and raise a family and plan a vacation and the thousands of other details involved with being a grown-up. Every one of these tasks requires learning and studying, and you've been a success at those things for years.

Now that you're in school you just have a different set of things to learn. But there are so many of them, and they are on such a restricted schedule, that you are going to have to polish your study skills to keep up. And to do that you will need some sort of strategy, a method that allows you to study most efficiently.

Develop a study method

If you had unlimited time, you could just learn everything there is to know about a given subject. Then you'd never have to worry about writing a paper or passing a test. And if you were one of the 18-year-olds who didn't have anything else to do, your study habits could be just awful and you would still probably manage to get through your classes. You would have lots of time to go back over the work, to rewrite the papers, etc., etc. And you'd have the energy to stay up nights on end cramming for exams and doing papers. I meet lots of those kids in my role as a college adviser.

You don't have that kind of time - or energy - to spare. And you can't afford to be making a lot of mistakes. You have to be able to absorb the material the first time you read it in most cases. Your papers and reports have to be pretty much dead on the first time you do them. And you have to be able to blow through those homework assignments just as fast and as accurately as you can.

This is a practical book, hopefully full of practical advice. Here's some about studying: you don't need to learn everything in a given course. You only need to learn what you are going to be tested on or the material necessary to write a convincing paper. Everything else is superfluous to earning that credit. That's not what a lot of academics would like to hear – especially from someone like me who earns part of his living from teaching and advising! – but it's the truth.

How do you find out what you need to learn? It should be on your syllabus or course information sheet. That schedule should tell you which chapters in your book or outside readings, movies, plays, videos etc. you will be covering.

Or your teacher will tell you, either flat out in class, or by signaling it to you by the amount of time and attention they give it. In many classes there will not be enough time in the semester to cover everything in your text. Or your teacher may decide that certain parts of your text are not worthy of study, and she will substitute other materials for those.

In most classes you won't need to read the textbook word-for-word. Use the review questions or sample tests at the end of the chapters (most textbooks have these) to test your comprehension and guide you to the important points in the chapters.

Simply put, don't spend much time studying materials that you won't be tested on. They will probably make interesting background material for the rest of the course. And you should probably scan those chapters quickly. But you shouldn't devote a lot of your precious time to them because they are simply not that important to your final grade.

> **"The kids don't really stay away from me when I'm studying. They're in and around there, and they can be pretty noisy at times. But I've learned - with the amount of kids that I have - to shut them out."**
> *Rich B., 44, has six children.*

How much time do you need to study?

Once you have determined what it is that you have to study, the next step is to figure out how long it is going to take you to do that studying. There is a convenient rule of thumb that can get you started with this computation: allocate three hours of outside studying for every hour of class.

If you are taking two classes per semester, you will probably be in school roughly six to eight hours per week. Note that classes with labs will probably meet more hours than the credit hours indicate. A four credit chem class, for example, will probably actually have you in school six or seven hours a week. Use the actual meeting time to estimate study requirements, not the credit hour load.

Once you know how many hours a week you will actually be in class, triple or quadruple that number to get a <u>rough</u> gauge of how much time school is going to absorb, both in-class time and study time. So a 6-hour, two-class schedule would mean you are going to have to find at least 18 to 24 hours per week. That includes the time you will actually spend in class.

This number is only roughly accurate, and is going to vary - perhaps quite a bit - for every person and every class. You can refine this a bit by figuring out how fast you read. Read ten pages of your text and time yourself. But don't just blow through the pages: this is not a race. Read the material carefully, underlining, highlighting or taking notes as required. Think about what you are reading. Ask yourself questions about what you are reading.

How long did it take you? If your text is 400 pages long - pretty typical, by the way - and it took you 20 minutes to thoroughly read and understand 10 pages, 400 pages is going to be 40 times longer, or 800 minutes, or slightly more than 13 hours.

But that assumes you are fresh, rested, alert and there are no interruptions. None of those will always be true. And you would never read 400 pages straight through anyway. You can probably safely double that number to take up the slack and compensate for wasted time, flagging concentration, ringing phones, whiney children, insistent spouses and so forth. (As an aside, note that most people can only concentrate for about an hour or so on any given subject. Then they need a little break - a walk around the house, a cup of coffee, a quick conversation with someone else.)

So if you double your reading time from this little exercise, that's close to two hours a week right there. And you haven't made a single trip to the library, visited a single web page, researched a single citation, written a single paper, re-read any of your classroom notes before a test, or tried to analyze the material you've read to figure out what sort of questions might be on an exam.

You can quickly see that this can be a very time-intensive proposition. One you are going to have to carefully fit into the rest of your life.

> **"I'll wait until everyone's gone to bed and I'll sneak out into the living room with my book and I'll curl up on the couch with the lamp behind me and I'll read."**
> *Evelyn S. has two kids and a husband and went to school full time at the very end of her 25-year trip to her BA.*

Establish a studying schedule

About the first week of every semester you should spend a little time cuddled up with your personal calendar, trying to figure out what you will be doing when for the next fifteen or sixteen weeks. First, fill in actual class times. Don't forget to allow enough time to drive to school (if that's the way you're attending), find a place to park, get to your classroom, etc.

Then, take a long, close look at the syllabus for each class to determine how much reading there will be each week for each class. But before you start allocating time in your calendar for that - and you have to - consider <u>when</u> you might find the time to study.

Nearly every student interviewed for this book got up pretty early in the morning and studied for an hour or two before they started the rest of their day. The reasons varied: the kids were still in bed (and therefore quiet), they had more energy in the morning, they had to be to work early anyway so getting up an hour earlier didn't really matter. The point is pretty clear: time in the morning seems to be more convenient, quieter and made more easily available than time later in the day when all of your adult responsibilities like work and family kick in. It's a good tactic, and it worked well for these students. It will probably work for you too.

So you might want to plug that early AM time into your calendar as study time. If you get up early on Saturdays or Sundays you can also put in several hours then before there's much going on in the house. (I know you're going to want to sleep in, but get used to the idea of never having quite enough sleep, at least while school is in session.)

The next step in successful scheduling is to make sure that everyone knows about your schedule and agrees to respect it. Posting it on your office door, hanging it over the dining room table or penciling it in on the kitchen calendar can help keep everyone informed. However you let everyone else know, it's imperative that they agree to it.

Studying early in the morning when the rest of the household is still in the sack will be easy to sell because they won't care. But you will have to work to convince them that you can just shut your office door every night right after supper for several hours. Your kids, your spouse and maybe even your boss will want some of your time.

Formally scheduling study time makes you commit to doing it, and that's critically important for someone as busy as you are. Ad hoc studying never gets done and you'll start to slip further and further behind in class. If you are going to night school classes, try to devote an hour or so every night, after you return from class. The same tactic can be used for weekend classes. This is a good time to go over the notes you took in class and fill in those inevitable blanks. It's also a good time to get a head start on the next reading assignment.

Make sure that everyone understands that at certain times of the week you are just not going to be available. And then enforce that, absolutely and without question. It is critically important that you have this time to yourself. Make sure that everyone understands that!

To get that kind of cooperation you will probably have to make a formal, scheduled commitment to family activities....a movie with the kids or the spouse every few weeks, a trip to the zoo, parent-teacher conferences. Creating written schedules that everyone can see and anticipate will go a long way in creating the time that you need for study. And it gives children, especially, some needed structure and provides an objective lesson about responsibility.

> **"I study wherever I can. If I've got 10 minutes before I go to work, I'll open up a book and get started on something."**
> *Jason B., has four children, a full time job, a part time job and went to school full time.*

Create a study group

A common technique to make the most out of study time is to do it with a few others in your class. Once you've read the material, it can help a lot to review it with other students. Ask each other questions. Work together to understand the material more fully. Compare your classroom notes. Cover for one another if one of you has to miss a class for some reason by sharing notes and handouts and schedule changes. Review each other's papers and research. You are, after all, all in this together!

Although school is probably the most convenient place for study groups to meet, adult students often use the study group as a social mechanism by scheduling group activities at their homes. And being in a study group can get you more comfortable with the idea of group projects, a favorite teaching tool for instructors working with adult students.

Note taking

Note taking is a skill that you probably already have from sitting in those sometimes endless Dilbert-like meetings as a working adult. But even if you don't have much experience taking notes, it's fairly easy to learn. Good notes are <u>not</u> verbatim records of what was said. They are merely meant to be memory joggers, reminders of important points.

Some notes can be nothing more than a single word or a reference to a particular page in a text. Underlining and highlighting can be considered a form of note taking, but too much of that destroys its usefulness and also the value of the book if you ever want to sell it. Pretty soon <u>everything</u> on a page looks like it was important.

Notes can be taken in class, while the professor is covering the material and writing things on the blackboard or showing overheads or PowerPoint slides, or while group discussions are underway.

But notes can also be created after the fact, as a way of reinforcing what you just heard in the class. Notes can also be a form of shorthand for what you just read and want to remember.

The important thing about notes is that they are just that: notes. You are not trying to reinvent the text book here, or rewrite everything you ever learned about a subject. Notes should be short, selective, to the point and relevant to the material. Notes should only jog your memory: they shouldn't be a complete substitute for it.

Notes don't have to be written. They can also be recorded and played back. This is particularly useful if you are the type of person who responds more effectively to audible information rather than written information. Remember what your Learning Styles exercise revealed in Chapter 14? Recorded notes are also handy if you have to drive a long distance back and forth to class, as you can play them back in the car.

Recording your class

Some students may benefit from tape recording the entire classroom lecture or discussion and then playing it back to refresh their memories of what went on, and to use as an aid in refining their notes. This technique can work for you, particularly if it fits well with your learning style.

But a couple of caveats are in order. First, this absorbs a *lot* of extra time. You are effectively attending class twice. Most adult students simply don't have this kind of extra time. If you do, and this technique works for you, then try it. But before you do, you need your professor's permission to tape record the class. By law, his lecture and other classroom activities are officially owned by him, and he holds the copyright to those materials. As silly as it may sound, recording class without his permission is against the law. Instructors typically allow recording. But always ask first.

Take a study skills class at school

Most schools understand that studying and note taking are skills, just like driving a car or playing a trombone. Like any skill, these can be learned. And once the basic skill is learned, it can be enhanced with practice: the more you study or take notes, the better you'll get at it.

Your school probably has a course devoted to the finer points of studying and note taking and how to do them effectively. Short courses like these are commonly offered to adults returning to school. Many of these courses are offered at night or on weekends when they're convenient for working adults, and they usually last only a few hours or so.

Find that study skills course and take it, even though it probably doesn't earn you any credit. You will start getting a return on that small time investment very quickly, and it will more than pay for itself over the years you are in school.

> **"I tried to allot between 8 to 10 hours of study time for each course per week. That includes the reading and writing papers. But it didn't include coming back and doing research in the library."**
>
> *Kathleen C., 56, worked full time and completed her degree exclusively through night school.*

CHAPTER 27

Writing

> "I wrote more papers for this Math class than for any English class I've ever taken. It was a writing intensive course. It was unbelievable."
> *Jason B. earned his Associate's degree and went on for his Bachelor's.*

There's good news and bad news in this chapter

If you're not much of a writer, this is the bad news: Your entire college career is going to be filled with writing assignments. It will be a rare course that will not require you to write something, and the majority of courses, even those which are not writing intensive, will require at least some writing. If you can't write reasonably well, it is going to be harder to get through college.

For that matter, if you can't write reasonably well, it will be harder than it should be just to get through life. Good writing is a very valuable skill that can be used in many ways in many areas of your life and work.

The good news
Schools understand the importance of being able to write well, and most of them are prepared to offer you a considerable amount of assistance to help you learn how to do it better.

Many colleges offer basic, intermediate and advanced classes designed to prepare you to take Freshman-level writing courses. These pre-Freshman classes usually carry no credit, and you will normally be charged for them. But they offer the opportunity to get up to speed on the basic writing skills you will need for the rest of your college career.

Do you need one or more of these classes? Most schools require new registrants to take a writing skills test of some kind that reveals how well they write, and, if they don't write well, what specific problems they might have. Once you take this test, the school will tell you if you need to attend a pre-Freshman writing skills class.

If you somehow miss taking this writing placement test, your writing skills will be judged in the beginning writing course you will certainly have to take. That course is often called English 100 or 101, or Freshman Writing, English Composition, College Composition, Basic Composition or something similar.

The writing teacher for that class should give you early feedback on whether your writing abilities are good enough to pass the basic writing course. These writing instructors often function as the guard at the gate for all the other courses in the school which require writing ability - and there are a lot of those courses. So these teachers are usually pretty blunt when it comes to telling their students that the student should probably drop the basic writing class and go back to one of the pre-credit preparatory writing classes.

> "I know that I don't have to spend time studying to take tests. But I also know that it's a reading and writing intensive college."
> Rich B. commenting on his non-traditional, non-residential college where earned his Bachelor's.

Writing can be learned

Some people have a natural talent for writing. The majority of us don't. We have to work at writing, and for most of us it is hard, painful work. Take some consolation in that fact. Even for those of us who do it for a living, it is not usually a whole lot of fun. Like you, we struggle to find the right word. We wonder what the next sentence should say. We have to think - hard - about how to put a coherent outline together. And most of us do not look forward to having to write several hundred or thousand words.

No matter where you go to school, you will almost certainly have to take at least one – and possibly more - beginning writing courses. These Freshman-level classes will probably be prerequisites for a lot of other classes, so you don't have much choice about taking them. Or about passing them. You simply have to.

And you will probably have to take them your first semester. Many schools require English Composition be taken as one of the very first classes.

If you don't pass those beginning courses, you will probably not be able to make it though college. It's that simple.

But nearly anyone can be taught the basics of good, clear writing. If it doesn't come naturally to you, you will have to work hard at it. Plan on rewriting and rewriting and then rewriting again. (The professionals do that all the time too.) But almost everyone can pass the beginning writing courses if they are willing to work hard enough at it.

If the idea of writing letters and papers and reports terrifies you - and it scares a lot of people - you should probably take only the beginning writing course your first semester and not take any other courses. This will allow you to spend as much time as necessary on learning (or re-learning) the basics of writing. It will be time well spent, because it will make you a better writer. And that will make the writing in your future courses easier.

Find the writing center and use it

Somewhere in your college there is probably something called the Writing Center, or the Writing Lab or the Writing Workshop. It is a special facility staffed by people whose only job is to help you construct and fine tune written assignments for your classes. This extra help is normally built into the price of your courses - they usually don't charge extra for it. And the people who staff writing centers are normally excellent writers themselves and understand the writing process thoroughly.

There are ways to increase your writing skills - exercises and assignments that concentrate on certain areas of writing like sentence and paragraph construction, outlining, punctuation, proofreading, etc. The Writing Center staff can help you analyze the problems you are having with your writing and give you exercises to strengthen these weak areas.

If you are having problems writing, or just need to brush up your skills a bit, visit your Writing Center. That's what it's there for.

> "I'm writing papers now that are <u>my</u> papers. ...With this gain in confidence I've been able to bring more of what myself is to my work. (I) put more of my thoughts into what I write."
>
> *Patrick A. worked nearly full time while in school. He earned his Bachelor's in about five years.*

What to do if you aren't much of a writer

Re-read the last section. Visit the Writing Center. Let your teachers know if you aren't comfortable with writing. Most of them will try to help you, but you have to be willing to help yourself.

If writing has always been a problem, avoid the writing intensive courses. These usually carry a special designation in the course description. If in doubt, ask your adviser or someone in the department that sponsors the class.

Writing Intensive courses

And a final bit of good news to end this chapter. Studies show that most people learn better and more by writing information out rather than taking fill in/multiple choice tests. The thinking processes involved in writing use more valued skills and involve more critical thinking. To allow students to take advantage of this, many colleges offer a curriculum called Writing Intensive or Writing Across the Curriculum. What this means is that a number of courses have had their writing component beefed up to require considerably more writing than would normally be the case.

As an example, a normal Biology 101 class might require only a single short report, with the major emphasis on conventional tests. The Writing Intensive Bio 101, on the other hand, might require several papers, lab reports, a final term paper and a few short tests.

A typical Writing Intensive program might require you to take 10 to 20 writing intensive courses out of the 40 or so you will need for your Bachelor's degree. You can see that a Writing Intensive curriculum concentrates on different kinds of work.

And these courses can complicate your planning, sometimes considerably, because if you are in a Writing Intensive program you must complete all of the requirements of that program to get the benefit. Writing Intensive courses are often harder to fill than the plain vanilla courses that they parallel, so they are often harder to find on the published class schedule.

And what is the benefit of all this extra work and more difficult planning? Usually you will be awarded a special degree that says, right on it: Writing Intensive. The physical piece of paper you get will note that, and so will your transcript.

What good is that? These days, with employers screaming about how poorly employees and job seekers write, it will probably be very valuable. A Writing Intensive concentration puts you in a very select group of graduates. And it should make you much more valuable to an employer.

If your school offers a Writing Intensive option, your adviser will have all the details. If you select this program, be prepared to work harder than you normally would. And be prepared to have to juggle your schedule more than you normally would, because the courses will not be as available. But if you are that good a writer, all of that extra work and planning will probably pay off in the long run.

"I just got a B+ on a paper and it's my last semester and I've worked so hard to raise my GPA from a B+ that a B+ wasn't good enough. So I'm doing a rewrite."

Evelyn S. graduated with her Bachelor's degree and a 3.5 GPA.

CHAPTER 28

Taking And Passing Tests

> "This semester I'm studying more. I'm having a real hard time with Biology. It's just not my forte. I got a 94 in my Cost Accounting exam the other night, but only a 2.5 out of 10 in my Bio exam. Oh, good! I'm not even an F - I'm a G!"
>
> *Lorene K. finished her Associate's degree and went on for her Bachelor's.*

Tests of some sort are a fact of life in college

Every student, young or old, faces them in every class. In high school there were only a couple of variations of test methods: multiple choice, fill in the blanks, short or long essay, and book reports and research papers covered most of the possibilities.

As we saw in a previous chapter, adults learn differently than younger people, and most teachers who deal with adults understand that tests should be more tailored to the adults' different learning style. So in addition to the tried and true test techniques just noted, in classes full of adults you are likely to run into a couple of other types of testing protocol as well.

Keep in mind the whole purpose of education. It is to learn. The teacher is being paid to help you do that, but she has to know that you actually are learning, and she needs you to be able to show it. If you can't show that you understand the material, you won't pass the course. The goal of all tests is to demonstrate mastery of the material being covered in class. And multiple choice and fill-in-the-blanks quizzes are only one way to demonstrate that learning. And perhaps not the best way for adults to demonstrate it.

A brief note on the life of the teacher

A typical class might have 20 to 30 or more students. Multiply that by the number of tests that will be given. If there's a quiz every two weeks in a 16-week class, a mid-term and a final for 30 students, your teacher has to review and grade 10 tests per student, or 300 different tests. That's a lot of work and responsibility right there. If she's teaching more than one class - and most full-timers teach at least three and as many as six per semester - you can see that the work load quickly gets pretty substantial.

Some types of tests can be graded by machines, essentially special purpose computers that do nothing but grade tests. These will often include some sort of "IBM card" where the answers to the questions are filled in with a #2 pencil. These are always multiple choice or true false tests. Anything more complex needs to be graded by a real person.

Note that many larger schools with graduate programs often use graduate students or TAs (Teaching Assistants) to supervise and grade tests. This can substantially decrease a professor's work load and by doing so, may actually increase the complexity of the test.

What does this discussion have to do with tests? Only that most teachers try to simplify their lives as much as they are able while still creating tests that will demonstrate that you really do know the material. Most teachers are not trying to "trick" you, or create inordinate amounts of work for you. Or for themselves, for that matter. This is particularly true in schools (like community colleges) where the teachers themselves supervise and grade the tests, rather than farming the task out to graduate student assistants. The teachers are simply asking you, by way of the test, what you have learned in their class.

This basic principle is important to keep in mind when thinking about tests. Teachers are human beings just trying to do their job in the most straightforward way possible. They do not purposely create overly complex testing schemes because they have to grade them. And if they have to spend an extra half hour on each test, for each student, the extra hours quickly begin to add up. Just like you, these people have personal lives and families outside of school. They really do attempt to keep testing at the minimum level necessary.

And all teachers, in all schools, are subject to the scrutiny of what are called "assessment" teams or standards. This essentially asks the question: what have our students learned? Assessment is a very big deal in most schools, and teachers have to demonstrate that students have learned some minimum amount of knowledge in their class. One way to do this is by tests and a review of the scores of those tests.

> "One of the things we get here is that adult student disease (known as) A-itis. If they don't get an A they're a failure. Anything less is unacceptable - they want a bullseye every time."
>
> *Betty Smith, adult student counselor at Monroe Community College in Rochester, NY, commenting on the standards adult students set for themselves. Betty is something of an expert on this subject, since she didn't start college until she was in her late 40s. She ultimately earned a Master's Degree.*

Hands-on tests

It's well known that adults learn best those things that they participate actively in, rather than passively listening to a lecture. That's why, in classes that lend themselves to the method, more "hands on" tests are a possibility. These might include presentations, demonstrations or the creation of something tangible - a model, a painting, a poem, a short story, a video tape, an example of some sort. These projects involve you physically in the material, and make you actually demonstrate, through the creation of something, that you really grasp the content of the class and the purpose of learning it.

The benefit of these sorts of tests is that they generally are a lot more fun than staring at multiple choice questions, and at the end of the class you have something that you can keep and show off - a painting, a model, a poem, a PowerPoint presentation, etc.

Since these projects usually take a fair amount of time to create (if you do them well), and your teacher knows this, they might count for a lot of your grade. In some ways this simplifies your life in that class. You only have to do one (or maybe two) relatively "big" things to pass that class. Instead of being constantly concerned with a continuous string of smaller quizzes, tests and papers, you have just one or two things you need to accomplish and you have met the criteria to demonstrate a knowledge of the material.

You still have to do the work, of course. And you have to do it pretty well to get a passing grade. But this sort of a testing strategy means you only have to keep track of a very small number of due dates on your cramped schedule. And you can probably work on the project a little bit here and there, instead of having to sweat the arrival of the quiz next week or the mid-term about halfway through the semester.

Group/team projects

In many real world circumstances we humans work in groups. Certainly this is true in the business world that many of us inhabit. As adults we have to learn to cooperate with other adults, set mutually acceptable goals, divide the work load among the participants, continually coordinate the different tasks, and gauge the progress of the project.

In many adult-oriented classes you may have the chance to work as a group on a project, a paper, a test of some sort. There are both plusses and minuses in these team projects.

The upside is that you get to split the work load with others. You don't have to do everything by yourself. And as in the real world, certain individuals are better at certain tasks than others. Some of your teammates will be better researchers, better organizers, better writers, better proofreaders, etc. Once you identify who is good at what, different members can be assigned different responsibilities and the whole team benefits. At least that's the theory.

The downside of working in teams is that you may have limited control over either the content or the quality of the project. You have to depend on the skills and responsibility of people who are essentially strangers to you. And, since most groups working on a project agree to accept a single grade for every member of the group, you are putting much of the responsibility for your grade into the hands of other people.

Does this make you nervous? It should at least give you pause for reflection. If you can exercise control over the make-up of the group, and have some confidence in the ability of everyone in the group to pull their own weight, then a group project may prove to be a benefit to you (and everyone else on the team.) But be warned that classrooms, just like workplaces and families, have their share of people who would just as soon you did all the work while they get to share in the credit.

Group projects can and do work very well in the classroom. And many teachers use them. But you need to be aware that they do not always work well, and that students and teachers alike are sometimes disappointed in the results. On several occasions I have personally had to break up confrontations between team members that were close to becoming physical, and loud, rather aggressive discussions seem to occur somewhat regularly in the teams in my classes.

The overall point here is that the decision to participate in a group project is optional in many classes, and you shouldn't just jump into one without some thought. Balance the risks and the rewards before you decide one way or the other.

> "I've had to read the whole text book, do all the questions in the text book, read three outside books, report on those books, and then do a 25 to 45 page paper."
> *Rich B. commenting on how he was tested in his non-residential, non-traditional four year college.*

Our old friends the multiple choice, true-false, matching, fill in the blanks, and short and long essay tests

We are all familiar with the multiple choice, true-false and matching tests from our days millions of years ago in high school. These test formats have a couple of things going for them if you are the teacher.

First, they are very simple to grade. Most schools even have machines that will grade these sorts of tests, or a template that can be given to nearly anyone to use to grade. They are easy to administer, usually don't take much time, and give the teacher a rough idea of how much of the material his students are absorbing.

But it is only a rough idea, for it allows students to basically memorize material without having any real understanding of it. It is easy to recall that the Battle of Hastings was in 1066 without knowing anything about what that battle meant, who fought in it, or how it may have changed the course of British and ultimately, world history. It is simple to remember that the water molecule has two hydrogen atoms and one oxygen atom without knowing the first thing about chemical reactions or valences.

Even though these three forms of tests leave a lot to be desired in terms of their ability to judge true learning, they are in widespread use simply because they are easy to create, administer and grade. So you should probably understand something about how to maximize your chances for good grades on them.

Multiple choice tests typically have a question followed by three, four or five potential answers. The most important piece of advice about these types of questions is this: read the question carefully. Some multiple choice questions are simple, the correct answer is immediately obvious and requires virtually no thought. They are perhaps put on the test just to give everyone a little credit, no matter how much they actually know. Tackle these first and get them out of the way.

On questions that are harder, you can usually count on one choice being so obviously wrong that it can be quickly eliminated as a possibility. A good strategy for dealing with the remaining choices is to try to formulate an answer to the question without looking at the choices. Then see if your answer matches any of them. Read the question and then read the first answer to see if that combination makes any sense. Then try the rest of the question-answer combinations. Often one of them will trigger a memory.

Questions which include absolutes such as "always," "never," or "every" can be tricky, because situations where these words are true are rare. "All of the above" and "none of the above" choices are often not the right choice either. Remember that all of the choices (or none of the choices) have to be true for this answer to be correct. And finally, never leave a question unanswered. Guess if you have to, but always choose an answer. You have a one in three or one in four or one in five chance of being right just by sheer chance.

True-false questions are not particularly popular with teachers, simply because you have a fifty-fifty chance of being correct just by guessing. But if you do run into a T-F question, remember that the odds are one in two that you'll get it right, even if you are clueless about what the correct answer is. Since you probably have at least some knowledge about the subject matter, your odds are better than that. One of the choices will probably look more correct than the other.

Matching questions can be tricky, especially if you don't read the directions carefully. You may be asked to match items that are different or opposite one another, rather than match things which are the same. As with multiple choice, do the easy matches first. This gets some of the clutter out of the way, gives you a sense of confidence, and saves some time. And by eliminating some answers, it increases the odds that you can simply guess n the remainder of the answers and be correct.

Short essay questions are fairly popular with teachers. They are relatively easy to grade since they are short, but because they require the student to actually explain something rather than check a box or fill in a blank, they offer the teacher a better gauge of the student's depth of knowledge.

Answers to short essay questions need to be just that: short and to the point. You don't have the option to ramble on here, hoping that the teacher will confuse quantity with quality. You need to demonstrate that you understand the topic and can extrapolate from general to specific knowledge. Use examples whenever possible, and draw conclusions. "The Battle of Hastings in 1066 changed European (and world) history because....." "Hydrogen and Oxygen combine easily to form the water molecule because...." "Hemmingway is recognized as a great writer because...."

Long essay questions can be thought of as more detailed versions of short essay questions, and to some extent that is true. But because they are longer, they require a much deeper understanding of the material, and probably better writing and organizational skills. Perhaps the best way to learn to cope with long essay questions is to review what other students have written. You teacher may make these available if you ask, or perhaps there are some on file in either the department office or in the library. Students who have already taken the class can be another source of old essay questions. You will need to look at both good essays and bad ones, and you need to recognize what makes one essay a success while another is a failure.

> **"She's not concise about what should be on the test. She gives us information about what's not on the test. And then there's things on the test that she hasn't even gone over yet."**
> *Jason B. making an observation on the vagaries of teachers and tests at the college where he earned his Associate's degree.*

Walter and Siebert, in their book *Student Success*, give eight tips on how to answer a long essay question. This is the most succinct summation I've seen on this topic, and it is right on the money. Here's what they say:

1. Read the questions carefully
2. Outline your answers
3. Use an introduction
4. Define your terms
5. Use subheads
6. Use examples and facts to support your main points
7. Draw conclusions; and
8. Allow time to review and edit your essay.

This book is probably worth buying just for their advice on essay questions, which is detailed and very helpful.

After the test
Tests can be very nerve-wracking, and most adult students dread them. You can't avoid them, however, so you have to prepare yourself to do the best you can, take the test and get on with the rest of class.

But after you take the test and the grade is back, you should probably chat a bit with your instructor about that test, regardless of what kind of grade you received. Try to find out how you can improve your test-taking style or why you went wrong in certain areas. Don't try to get the teacher to change your grade: it's a tacky request that will just make you look bad. Your long-term interest here is in learning, and getting a better handle on your test-taking skills can help you do that.

Review old tests

Many teachers or departments will make available previously used tests for review. If your teacher does this, take them up on the offer! By making old tests available, they are trying to give you a VERY big hint about what might be contained on your tests. And while the questions probably won't be identical, they will probably flag the things that this teacher thinks are important. That will give you a good head start in determining what to study. And that can save you a lot of time and increase your chances for a better grade.

If your teacher doesn't offer to share previous tests, ask why not. It may just be an oversight, or something no one has ever asked about. All she can say is no. But if she won't make them available, perhaps students who have taken her class in the past might still have their copies available.

> **"If it's multiple choice or true-false or short answer, I can do those. But if it's essays, I have to have a computer."**
> *Deanne L. is disabled with repetitive motion injury. That didn't stop her from graduating with a 3.76 GPA.*

Ask for a different testing strategy - you might be surprised

Adults learn differently than younger students. And adults learn differently from each other, as you discovered when you took the Learning Styles Inventory in Chapter 14. Given that fact, you might be confronted with testing styles that you are just not comfortable with.

Perhaps you simply don't do well with multiple choice or fill-in tests, but are much better with essays. Maybe you'd rather do a hands-on project or deliver a demonstration in front of the class. Perhaps some extra reading and some book reports are more your style. Maybe group projects make you a little nervous, and you'd prefer to work by yourself. Or vice versa.

However you learn, it never hurts to ask your instructor if they could accommodate a different testing strategy. Is there another way that you could demonstrate that you've learned the material? All they can say is no.

> **"One evening an adult student came to me and said, I haven't been able to sleep the last few nights. I dreamed that I got a B in a course. Oh? What does that mean, I asked. She said, well, I've got a perfect 4.0 average. I dreamed I got a B. It was a nightmare!"**
> *Bill Sigismond, head of the Office of Experiential and Adult Learning at Monroe Community College in Rochester, NY, commenting on the standards adults often set for themselves in college.*

CHAPTER 29

Personal Computer, Yes Or No?

> "I bought one two semesters ago. I was in a Statistics class and I found that I was in school in the computer lab 20 hours a week. ....So I went out and bought a computer after the class. I said, this is crazy. I need to be home doing this work."
> *Jason B. on his decision to get a personal computer.*

The personal computer has completely revolutionized the way many of us work

It allows us to do some things much more quickly and accurately than was possible just a decade or so ago. And it allows us to do some things that just weren't possible at all.

If you can afford a personal computer, buy it. If you don't use it for anything except writing papers and accessing the huge amount of information available on the Internet, it will pay for itself in time saved. You won't have to retype pages on a typewriter for the sake of a single mistake. You won't have to drive back to school to use the campus computer center to get work done. You'll be able to work on papers on your schedule, rather than someone else's. And in many cases you will be able to eliminate or shorten trips to the library for research, by hooking up to the Internet and the billions of pages of information on the World Wide Web.

**Computers are getting
less expensive all the time**

My first computer was an Apple IIe, bought in 1982. It cost me a fortune, had no hard drive, 64k (yes, k) of RAM, and you had to load the operating system from a floppy disk every time you wanted to use it. It changed my life as a writer. Gone was carbon paper, white out, time-consuming error correction and retyping. It was one of the most important things I've ever bought. I cannot imagine life without a personal computer. And I certainly cannot imagine life as a college student without a computer.

Somewhere in your town there is a retailer who sells used computer systems. One of the largest in the country is Computer Renaissance (http://www.compren.com/locations/index.asp), but there are others. Stores handling new computers often sell used ones too, and they may carry a warranty.

Or, if you trust your judgment, look in your local newspaper's classifieds or on eBay or another auction site. You can probably get a decent used personal computer for a few hundred dollars. This won't buy you the latest, flashiest technology, but you should be able to get a sturdy, functional machine that will allow you to use a word processing program, hook you up to the Internet and your school's computer system, and run some other useful software like spreadsheets, games, home accounting, etc.

> "The reason I waited this long to go to college is word processing."
> *Patrick A. had a smile on his face when he said this.*

As I write this, new personal computers are being advertised for less than $600, and if the past is any guide, you can expect prices to continue to drop.

There are two main types of personal computers: the DOS-based Windows™ operating system popularized by Microsoft (www.microsoft.com) and the Apple Macintosh™ (www.apple.com) operating system. What you get depends on what you are going to be using it for. Either will do a fine job on word processing, spreadsheets, games and so forth, and both types are easy to connect to the World Wide Web and Internet. Engineers, science and math types will probably want a DOS-based system to maintain compatibility with the systems they likely use at work. People doing graphics, writing, photo manipulation, illustration, animation, brochure, magazine or book design, publishing, Web page design and similar tasks will probably want a Mac, as that system is pretty much the standard in those industries.

Whatever you get, make sure you have a decent word processing program. Microsoft Word™ has become the de facto standard in the business world, but there are several others just as good and less expensive. As a student you don't need all the bells and whistles that a high end program like Word offers. A simpler, cheaper, easier to learn program will do the job, and will be much easier to use.

As noted in another chapter, going to college means a lot of writing. Many teachers require papers to be typewritten - they just won't accept handwritten assignments. (If you had to read a hundred or more different types of handwriting every semester, you wouldn't want to either.) Since that's the case, make it easy on yourself. A decent WP program allows you to quickly and neatly make changes in papers, move entire chunks of thought around, do revisions, etc.

And the papers themselves can be dressed up a bit through the use of different typefaces and styles like *italics*, **bold type** and so forth. Presentation <u>does</u> make a difference in how teachers react to papers. And although that is not a substitute for good, clear writing, a neat, well produced paper will almost always get a better grade than one that is sloppily typed.

Printers have come down in price to the point where they are almost throw-away items. You can buy a very nice <u>color</u> ink jet printer from a world class company like Hewlett-Packard (www.hp.com) or Epson (www.epson.com) for less than $100, in some cases much less. Printers are so inexpensive that they are often included free with the purchase of a computer.

A good printer increases the visual quality of your work even more, and the judicious use of color, in addition to type styles, can make a difference in the reaction your paper gets.

Modems and higher speed Ethernet connections are now pretty standard in new computers. These allow easy connection to the Internet and World Wide Web, and can save you countless hours of searching the stacks in your school or local library.

Personal computers have now become home appliances, and although they're not a cheap as toasters (yet), they are about as necessary. This is particularly true for students. If you can at all afford one, get it. You'll never regret the investment.

> **"I'm a walking anachronism, I'm afraid. High tech for me is a ball point pen. ....I used the typewriter all the way through. Now that I've learned my lesson I'm going to get a computer."**
> *Dave P. earned his Bachelor's degree from a non-traditional college.*

CHAPTER 30

Day Care

> "Right now our 5 month old is in day care. It's $125 a week. I drop her off, my wife picks her up."
> Kevin R.

One of the largest single identifiable groups of older college students is parents

One estimate I saw said that 27% of undergraduates have children. A sizable number of these people are single parents - moms and dads trying to raise their kids without a partner. And where you find parents, you always find a need for safe, reliable, affordable day care, whether it's to cover working hours or class time.

Unfortunately, this need is not being met. In early 1998 supporters of a congressional drive to include child care funding in a higher education bill estimated that only 10 to 25 percent of students who could use campus-based child care were actually served by such programs. Several years later not much has changed: safe, affordable, convenient day care is still a challenge to locate. This leaves a lot of students wondering where to put the kids while they're in school trying to insure a better future for all of them.

This is a tough problem for a lot of students, single parents and married couples alike, and it takes ingenuity to solve it. Here are a few suggestions. Then I'm going to devote the rest of the chapter to a review of how actual students have solved their child care needs. There might be a few more ideas in those quotes.

School-based programs

A lot of schools have responded to the child care need, and not just for the sake of their students. Faculty and staff moms and dads also need a convenient place to stash the little ones while they are working. Many colleges now run full-scale day care centers right in their schools.

Does your school have one? You may have to do a little investigating to find out. I checked the catalogs of several colleges that I know for a fact run day care centers - and I didn't find any information in the catalogs.

I think I know why. Most of these day care centers are full, and the schools don't want to publicize the availability of a service that they can't really provide. Waiting lists for day care seem common. But even if there is a wait list, get on it.

The area around the campus

Also check around the neighborhood of the campus. There are a lot of single moms and dads going to college, and a lot of couples with one or both parents in school, and many of them need day care for their children while they are in class. It is possible that someone in the vicinity of the school has figured this out and has a facility that caters mostly to students. It can't hurt to look around. Campus bulletin boards may be a good place to start your search.

Relatives

Close family members are often the most supportive of efforts to go to college. Parents, siblings, uncles, aunts, grandparents - all might be willing to take a tour of duty watching your kids while you're in class. If child care is going to be a major issue in your return to school, you should probably involve your potential babysitters early in the discussion process.

Neighbors
Other moms or dads in your neighborhood, working or not, in school or not, often have the same concerns about child care as you do. Maybe one (or more) of them would be willing to watch your kids for a few hours while you're in class in trade for you watching theirs while they attend school, run errands or go to a movie or dinner.

Other students
Since every adult student with small children confronts the day care problem, there might be an opportunity to start a child care club with other students, with all of the parents taking turns.

An extension of this possibility is to approach the school administration to see if they would donate a room right on campus where adults could take their kids at no charge while they are in class. If all of the students dropping kids off agreed to spend an hour watching other kids in exchange for an hour of baby sitting by a fellow student, the club would be self-supporting in terms of having enough people to staff the room. Charging a very modest per hour/per kid amount would generate enough money to pay for things like snacks for the kids, toys or an occasional diaper. There is usually enough demand on campus for child care that this solution might have a chance of working.

However, there are also potential legal liability issues in this idea, and these days that might be reason enough for a school not to consider it.

Friends
Like neighbors, friends might be willing to watch little Suzy a few hours every week if you were willing to guard their little Joey in exchange. Or perhaps you could just pay them to baby sit.

How other students have solved the child care problem

Nearly every adult student interviewed for this book – and hundreds of students I've advised - had to find a safe, caring place for their kids while they were in class. Let's look at some of their solutions.

> **"(My wife and I) overlap. We pretty much have it down to Fridays, but it used to be three days a week. While my wife is teaching (music in our home) and I'm either at work or in school, we've had to cover a few hours here and there. We use her music students as a source of babysitters, teenage girls and boys. We only ask them for afternoons and only for a couple of hours. And we pay them pretty good because if you pay them enough they'll be reliable."**
> *Patrick A.*

"We have older children that watch the younger ones for us. They give us a little resistance about this, but they get perks."
Rich B.

"My oldest son watches my youngest son at night, when my husband isn't at home. And then I have a neighbor who babysits. (She's) a very good friend of mine. And we barter our day care. She has little ones and if she needs someone to watch them and I'm free, I watch them. So that's where (my youngest son) goes for about an hour in the mornings."
Deanne L.

"I've tried to schedule around the day care problem. On Thursdays my daughter is in Brownies and the Brownie leader invited her to come to her house after school on days when she had Brownies. And then on Tuesdays, when I had a Tuesday/Thursday schedule, she would go to another friend's house. And other times I'd pay day care. On Fridays my husband is off so he babysits."
Evelyn S.

"My oldest son is 9, so he's in school all day. My other son, we had him in day care but it was too expensive. He's 4. His mother has him during the day, and he spends a lot of time with my grandmother and with me. My other two children are with my wife. And there are times when I'll bring my kids to school. The professors here have been really, really good about it. My classmates are great. If I'm taking an exam or something, they'll take my son down to the gym. Or my daughter, she'll go down there with the basketball team and play basketball for an hour or two so I can take my test. I see kids here all the time."
Jason B.

"My mother watches my son. If I can, I'll bring him with me on any activities that I can, even in school if it's something that he can sit through. I remember when I was taking Philosophy of Education, he'd sit out in the hall. I'd bring a desk out of one of the rooms and he'd sit there and do his homework while I was in class. I'd have him so he was in view of the door, and at break time I'd go out and check on him. He'd do his homework, and he'd have books to read and games to play."
Helen D.

"We're fortunate because our girls are a little older. And we're also fortunate because I work at home. Before that, it was really hard because day care was costing $600 to $800 a month, two kids in day care. So when this opportunity to work at home came up....it saves tremendously on day care and makes scheduling a whole lot easier. So I work at night and take classes during the day."
Valerie G.

"This year it's costing me about $15 a week. That's the cheapest it's been. It's usually been $70 to $80 a week, especially when she was in kindergarten. Probably the toughest was the year I was going (to school) part time and working part time, she was in a pre-school that was like $700 for the year. Then I was paying $70 a week for the babysitter. It was costing me more than I was making, and I thought, My God! I think it was after that year, when she started kindergarten, that I decided it's time to go full time.

My neighbor across the street watches her now. She's a stay-at-home mom with four kids. It's great. My husband gets involved too. He picks her up on Tuesdays. He takes her to Brownies this year. And he's been a real help with getting her to activities and birthday parties and so forth."
Ann H.

"I try to arrange it so that one of my older children is there (to watch my 9 year old.) Once or twice I've had to take him with me to a couple of classes. Because I really don't have any backup. And if I couldn't do that, I would probably have to stay home with him. The older kids are pretty good about watching him. They realize this is a joint effort."
Karen D.

"I have a unique situation in day care in that about five years ago I built the house that I live in with my parents. We co-own the house. And part of that was to have somebody there when (my son) comes home from school. So that's really my back up."
Andrea W.

"Grandma watches the kids. Grandma puts them on the bus, and Grandma takes them off. I'm here (at school) until 5 or 6 o'clock, so she'll feed them so I don't have to. She's real good because she knows what we have to do for the day. She has a copy of our schedule so she can get them started. My mom and my sisters and brothers are a real big help too."
Joyce M.

CHAPTER 31

Do You Have Time For A Social Life?

> "I have a social life because it goes into the planner first."
> *Valerie G.*

> "Social life? What's that?"
> *Lorene K.*

The short answer to the question in the title of this chapter is: maybe

But if you do find time for a social life, it probably won't be like the social life you had before you started school. Remember the discussions about time management and studying? If you are taking just two classes a semester, you will probably be devoting 20 or more hours a week to school. Factor in those weeks where you have some really big commitment for school - a major paper or project due, studying for a final, meetings on a team assignment, etc. Now add in the amount of time that you work at your job. Include the time that you still need to devote to your family. And there's probably still some chores around the house and errands that need to be run that you can't hand off to another family member.

Does this look like the schedule of someone who has a full, active social life?

> "I have a real active social life. My children and I are heavily involved in our church. And we do things that the college has going on too. We find the time by scheduling. Very tight scheduling."
> *Joyce M., a single mother of three, attended school full time and worked 20+ hours a week.*

You'll need to schedule your social life now

It is still possible to have something like a social life. But it will be abbreviated. And it will have to be tightly scheduled, just like the rest of your life will be. The flexibility to have a real, adult-style social life, where events and functions can be spontaneous, is one of the major sacrifices you are going to have to make to be a successful adult college student. If you still want to do all of the things that you used to do, before you started school, you are going to be either disappointed when you find out you can't....or a failure in school when you try to still do them. That's the harsh reality. School is a major time user, and that time is going to have to come from somewhere. Your social life is going to be a major contributor.

It is still possible to have some social life. But you are going to have to be more creative about how you have it. Here are a few ideas that have worked for others.

> "My social life is during school breaks, semester breaks. That's when I do my socializing. When I have my breaks I meet my girlfriends for lunch. Other than that, most of them don't bother me when I'm taking classes. And I take time out on the weekends for my family, especially Sundays. Sunday is family day."
> Linda W.

Schedule your social activities during breaks

While it's possible to go to school nearly year round, and a lot of adult students do, most of them don't attend the Intersession crash courses. Although many do use the short, more intensive sessions held during the summer, they skip some every now and then just to maintain their sanity. These sessions are very tough, and people with families and jobs just find them too difficult and time-consuming. There are other ways to earn that credit that are more in line with the kind of life adults actually lead, and we've discussed them in this book.

So if you're not attending school during semester or summer breaks, what can you do? Some socializing is probably a good idea. The semester break is typically a month or so around Christmas and New Year's, and taking the summer off might add another three months. It should be possible to do a lot of things in those periods that were put on hold during the 30 - 32 weeks a year that you actually attend school.

> "The biggest problems have probably been just family time. Something has to give so we can just be a family. There are certain things that are the law. Like we eat dinner at 6 PM and everybody better be at the table. I can be in the middle of something and have some sort of a brainstorm for a paper, but everything gets dropped for dinner."
>
> *Ann H. uses dinner as a time to socialize with her family.*

Socialize with the family

In the Time Management chapter it was suggested that combining activities was one way to maximize your use of time. This is a good example of that. You owe your family some of your time, and you owe yourself some socializing. By combining them, you are effectively doing two things at once. Catch a movie together, go to that concert in the park, have a picnic. Family activities can also further build support for the time you spend with school, by allowing you to explain, in a relaxed setting, why it's so important that you go to college. Never pass up an opportunity to schmooze your family about the importance of college.

Use campus events for socializing

Colleges often sponsor social and entertainment events on campus. Plays, concerts, movies, poetry and book readings, athletic events and so forth are frequent, varied and usually priced right. Many are actually free! You might want to combine attendance at one of these with a family outing. It's usually cheap entertainment, and it gives your family a chance to see where you go to school. It's fun being a tour guide, and it further involves your family in your college life.

Campus events may also be used to get credit in classes. This is particularly true for humanities classes like English, Literature, Drama, Speech Communications and so forth. If there is an event on campus that looks like it might fit into the content of one of your classes, you may want to suggest to your instructor that she allow you to attend it and write a short report on it for credit.

> "By the second semester I had made some friends, I had met some other people who were in a similar situation as me. They were older, returning students. And I get along fine with the kids, too."
>
> *Evelyn S. started school in the mid-70s. About 25 years later she had her BA.*

Socialize with your fellow students

This will probably happen automatically. You're all in the same boat here, and your common interests will throw you together to some extent anyway. Even the younger students will probably turn out to be friends, once they get over their fear of you. (And yes, they are just as uncertain about you as you are of them.)

Socializing with other students gives you an audience for concerns and successes, an audience that understands you and what you are going through. Most adult students find that the friends they make in school become very good friends indeed.

> **"If you're not willing to make the commitment in terms of time, then it probably is not a good idea for that person to do. It requires sacrifices and I think you have to decide which things you're going to give up in order to do that."**
> *Andrea W. commenting on what it takes to be an adult student.*

CHAPTER 32

What Are You Waiting For?

> "I plan on going to school for the rest of my life. It's just been a great experience. It's just opened my eyes and made me realize that there's a whole other world out there that I just wasn't a part of."
> *Jason B., 27, father of four young kids, worked a full time job, a part time job and went to school full time.*

Just do it!

So, you've finished this book, and maybe you've looked through some of the other books like it. Now you know what to expect. You've learned many of the tricks and shortcuts that can get you through college in record time. And you've read about the strategies and tactics that other students just like you have used to get their degrees. You've met people who are working, who have families, who have social lives, who have all of the same adult responsibilities that you have.

The only difference is that they've figured out how to go to college while still maintaining all those other parts of their lives. You can too.

Go look in the mirror. I'll wait here.

Are you back? Good. What did you see?

I saw a college graduate, just waiting to get out. A tough, creative, adult student who knows that the biggest step is always the first one. Take that first step now. Check the Reference for more information if you need it, then use your Yellow Pages or the World Wide Web to find a college in your area. Call them to set up a counseling appointment with an adult student adviser.

Now. Do it right now. What are you waiting for? That college graduate is waiting to get out. Give yourself a hand.

Do it now.

> "There was nothing more petrifying than that first day experience of seeing everybody that was close to your children's age. And the first thing that I looked for was some person who resembled me. And I found some. It was wonderful."
>
> *Bette B., 40, married, working, mother of two teenagers, finished her Associate's and Bachelor's, and is on-track to earn a Master's.*

Reference

Other Sources of Information
Although I have tried to make this book a stand-alone reference for returning adult college students, there is a huge amount of information available from various sources that can be of real value. I referred to many of these in compiling this book.

These books and websites are just a small start on additional information. A Google search or a trip to Amazon.com, Barnes&Noble.com or any large on-line or bricks-and-mortar bookstore will yield hundreds more titles.

Books On Being An Adult Student
There is not a lot of information available that is specifically targeted to the adult college student. What is available is somewhat inconsistent in quality. You might find these books helpful.

Bruno, F. Arco Going Back to School: College Survival Strategies for Adult Students Arco Pub; 3rd Revision edition, June 2001.

Shields, C. Back in School: A Guide for Adult Learners. Hawthorne, NJ: Career Press, 1994.

Siebert, A. & B. Karr The Adult Student's Guide to Survival & Success. Practical Psychology Press; 5th edition, April 1, 2003.

Walter, T. & A. Siebert. Student Success. New York: Harcourt Brace, 1996.

Time Management:
Much of going back to college as an adult is a time management problem, one made all the worse by the very complex lives that adults lead. These books can help.

_____ Time Management: Increase Your Personal Productivity And Effectiveness (Harvard Business Essentials) Harvard Business School Press, 2005

Allen, D. Getting Things Done: The Art of Stress-Free Productivity Penguin, 2003

Davidson, J. et al The Complete Idiot's Guide to Managing Your Time. MacMillan Publishing Company; 2nd edition, January 1999

Ferner, J. Successful Time Management (A Self-Teaching Guide), 2nd ed. New York: John Wiley & Sons, 1995.

McCay, J. The Management of Time New York: Prentice Hall, 1995.

Morgenstern, J. Time Management from the Inside Out, second edition : The Foolproof System for Taking Control of Your Schedule--and Your Life, Henry Holt & Co., 2004

Panella, V. The 26-Hour Day: How to Gain at Least 2 Hours a Day with Time Control. Career Press; 1st edition, 2001.

Scharf-Hunt, D. Studying Smart: Time Management for College Students. New York: Harperperennial, 1990.

Financial Aid Information:
The Student Guide: Financial Aid. U. S. Department of Education, Washington, DC, 2003.

Finney, D. Financing Your College Degree. New York: The College Board, 1997.

How Adults Learn:
If you have an interest in how you learn, and how you are different from (and usually better than) younger students, these four books provide a solid foundation in this fascinating subject.

Cross, K. Adults as Learners. San Francisco: Jossey-Bass Publishers, 1981.

Hiemstra, R. & B. Sisco. Individualizing Instruction. San Francisco: Jossey-Bass Publishers, 1990.

Knowles, M. The Modern Practice of Adult Education. Englewood Cliffs, NJ: Prentice Hall Regents, 1980.

Adult Learning Methods. M. Galbraith, Editor. Malabar, FL: Krieger Publishing Company, 1991.

Selecting A Major and A School:
Your local bookstore has several shelves of books covering this topic. Since most of them are aimed squarely at the 18-year-old high school student, many of them may be of limited value to you. The ones listed below cover more general information and are probably more useful. Both Peterson's and the College Board publish a wide range of information about college in general, and you are likely to find books by both publishers at your local bookstore.

Peterson's Two-Year Colleges 2006/Four-Year Colleges 2006 (Peterson's Annual Guides to Undergraduate Study, 2006) -- by Peterson's Guides (Editor), Petersons Publishing; Paperback. (Two-volume set). Princeton, NJ: Peterson's Publishing, 2006.

The College Board Index of Majors & Graduate Degrees 2006: All-New Twenty-sixth Edition. New York: College Board Publications, 2005.

The College Board College Handbook 2006: All-New Forty-third edition. New York: College Board Publications, 2005.

Reference Books:
The first two are must-have books for anyone who does any writing - and college students all do a lot of writing. The MLA Handbook will show you how to structure research papers, bibliographies, etc. Strunk and White's is simply the best short book about writing ever written.

Gibaldi, J. MLA Handbook for Writers of Research Papers, 6th ed. New York: Modern language Association of America, 2003.

Strunk, W. Jr. & E. B. White. The Elements of Style. 4th ed. New York: Macmillan, 2000.

Turabian, K. <u>A Manual for Writers of Term Papers, Theses, and Dissertations</u>, 6th ed. Chicago: University of Chicago Press, 1996.

Study Guides:
This website offers literally hundreds of tips on a very wide variety of subjects related to studying:
http://www.studygs.net/

On-Line Resources

The number of things you can learn on the Internet is enormous. And while you won't want to abandon your school or local library, the Net is almost always a good place to start your research. Here are a few sites to get you started:

Adult Student Websites
www.adultstudents.com
www.educationforadults.com
www.adultstudentcenter.com/
www.back2college.com/
www.adultstudent.com/
http://adulted.about.com/
http://www.ecampustours.com/collegeplanning/adviceforadultstudents.aspx

Finding a Community College:
Try the American Association of Community Colleges at http://www.aacc.nche.edu. This site lists the membership of this national organization of community colleges - more than 1000 of the approximately 1100 in the country.

Financial Aid Information:
http://www.fafsa.ed.gov/
http://www.collegeboard.org/
http://www.finaid.org/
http://www.studentservices.com/fastweb/
http://www.collegenet.com/mach25/

Advanced Placement Tests:

http://www.collegeboard.org/ap/

Everything You Ever Wanted To Know About Education:
http://www.eric.ed.gov/
This is ERIC, the Educational Resources Information Center, a huge collection about virtually every aspect of education.

Libraries:
http://www.lib.washington.edu/
This site provides a link to the card catalogs of dozens of libraries worldwide, plus library-related companies.

Books:
http://www.amazon.com
This is the world's largest on-line bookstore, and can provide you access to several million books in print. It's easy to use, and a secure ordering system allows easy-on-line purchases.

Typical search keywords:
adult student, adult education, continuing education, education, distance learning, college student, returning to college, mature student, returning student, study, term paper, writing, college financing, grants, scholarships, career counseling, career change, education loans, financial aid, veteran's benefits, college, community college.

Using the Internet for School:
Guernsey, L., College.edu: <u>On-Line Resources for the Cyber-Savvy Student</u>, 4th ed. Alexandria, VA: Octameron Associates, 2000.

Organizations

National Home Study Council, 1601 18th Street, Washington, DC 20009.

College Level Examination Program, CN 6601, Princeton, NJ 08541

Proficiency Examination Program, American College Testing Program, PO Box 4014, Iowa City, IA 52433. (In New York State: POP, Regents College, 1450 Western Avenue, Albany, NY 12203).

DANTES Program, Mail Stop 3/X, Educational Testing Service, Princeton, NJ 08541.

Stanley Kaplan Educational Center, 810 Seventh Avenue, New York, NY 10019.

Other ways to get credit

Credit By Examination
College Level Examination Program (CLEP), Box 6600, Princeton, NJ 08543.

American College Testing Proficiency Examination Program (ACT-PEP), Box 168, Iowa City, IA 52243.

DANTES Standard Subject Tests, 6490 Saufley Field Road, Code 20A, Pensacola, FL 32509-5243.

Credit for Life Experience:
Council for Adult and Experiential Learning, 243 South Wabash Avenue, #800, Chicago, IL 60604.

Credit for Work Training:
American Council of Education's Program on Non-Collegiate Sponsored Instruction (ACE-PONSI), One DuPont Circle, Suite 250, Washington, DC 20036.

Credit for Military Training:
Service-members Opportunities College (SOC), One DuPont Circle, Suite 680, Washington, DC 20036.

Credit for Volunteer Work and Homemaker Skills:
Accrediting Women's Competencies, T-154, Educational Testing Service, Princeton, NJ 08541.

Evaluation of Previously Earned Credit:
Regents Credit Bank Service, 1450 Western Avenue, Albany, NY 12203.

Getting A Degree in an Other-Than Classroom Setting:
Bear, J. & M. Bear. <u>Bears' Guide to Earning College Degrees Nontraditionally</u>, 13th ed. Benicia, CA: C&B Publishing, 1999.

Bear, J. & M. Bear. <u>Bears' Guide to Earning Degrees by Distance Learning</u>, Ten Speed Press; 15th edition, 2003.

Bear, J. & M. Bears' Guide to College Degrees by Mail & Internet: 100 Accredited Schools That Offer Bachelor's, Master's, Doctorates, and Law Degrees by Distance Learning (College Degrees By Mail and Internet), Ten Speed Press, 9th edition, 2003.

Burgess, W. <u>The Oryx Guide to Distance Learning: A Comprehensive Listing of Electronic and Other Media-Assisted Courses</u>, 2nd ed. Oryx Press, 1997.

Dixon, P. <u>Virtual College</u>. Princeton, NJ: Peterson's Publishing, 1996.

<u>Kaplan Guide to Distance Learning</u>. New York: Simon & Schuster, 1997.

<u>Peterson's Guide to Distance Learning Programs</u>, 6th ed. Princeton, NJ: Peterson's, 2003.

<u>Peterson's Independent Study Catalog</u>, 7th ed. Princeton, NJ: Peterson's Publishing, 1998.

Veteran's Information

To request copies of your military records, including discharge papers and information on military training, contact:

National Personnel Records Center, Military Personnel Records, 9700 Page Blvd., St. Louis, MO 63132-5100

This agency prefers that requests for records be submitted on the Veteran's Administration Standard Form 180, available from the VA. Requests can also be made by letter. Include your full name, signature, branch of service, your service number, social security number, and your dates of service.

This VA Standard Form 180 is available on the internet on the VA site at: http://www.va.gov/forms/dot/SF180.dot

or

http://www.archives.gov/st-louis/military-personnel/standard-form-180.html

You can contact the VA by phone at a variety of different numbers, depending on what your topic is. Check this web site for those numbers:

https://iris.va.gov/phonenbrs.asp

If you have Internet access, the Veteran's Administration has extensive information available here: http://www.va.gov/

For purposes of determining if you are eligible for benefits associated with a specific conflict, these are the approximate dates:

Persian Gulf Conflict: on or after August 2, 1990
Vietnam War: December 22, 1961 to May 7, 1975
Korean War: June 27, 1950 to January 31, 1955
World War II: December 7, 1941 to December 31, 1946
World War I: April 6, 1917 to November 11, 1918
Mexican Border Period: May 9, 1916 to April 5, 1917
Spanish-American War: April 21, 1898 to July 4, 1902

You may also qualify if you participated in:

Lebanon: June 1, 1983 to December 1, 1987
Grenada: October 23, 1983 to November 21, 1983
Panama: December 20, 1989 to January 31, 1990

As of this writing we are still in Afghanistan and Iraq.

Note that these dates are approximate. Your state may define them differently, or Congress may have redefined them since this book was published. Any change in dates may affect your eligibility for any benefits available.

Your official dates of service will appear on your DD-214 discharge papers. If you can't locate your DD-214, contact the Personnel Records Center in St. Louis mentioned at the beginning of this section.

For Alleged Violations of the Family Rights and Privacy Act referred to in Chapter 24, write to:

Family Policy Compliance Office
U. S. Department of Education
400 Maryland Avenue SW
Washington, DC 20202-4605

Printed in the United States
105957LV00002B/277-300/A